A Matter of Self-confidence - Part II

An introduction to self-confidence coaching in a book

Also by Elizabeth J Tucker:

Simply Stress (Stress Management Exercises, Strategies and Techniques)

The 7 Deadly Sins of Chairing Meetings (Let's Get it Right Every Time)

The 5 P's For a Perfect Meeting (A Step-by-step Guide to Navigate Meetings Like a Pro)

Success Starts Here (Things Every Minute Taker Should Know)

Books by Eliza-Jane Jackson:

Why Doesn't The Law Of Attraction Work?

Creating Prosperity and Abundance

Create Your Own Prosperity Wheel (A step-by-step guide to using The Law of Attraction to manifest the things you want!)

Publisher: Shepherd Creative Learning

Publisher's Note:

A Matter of Self-confidence - Part II
An introduction to self-confidence coaching in a book

Author: Elizabeth J Tucker

Publisher: Shepherd Creative Learning
Year of Publication: 2017

Copyright:

First Printing: 2015
Second Printing: 2016
Third Printing: 2017

ISBN: 978-0-9931145-2-6

Publisher: Shepherd Creative Learning

(www.shepherdcreativelearning.co.uk)

Book cover designed by Tristan King - V o o d o o   D e s i g n
(www.voodoodesignshropshire.com)

Dedication:

The book is dedicated to Dennis Shepherd, Rosemary and Geoffrey Tucker and Richard and Minna Jackson. All have now moved onto a bigger and better place, but I'm sure they're still with me.

Thanks also to Hugh Price (my funny, inspiring and supportive cousin). 'A Matter of Self-confidence' is the result of one of our deep and meaningful kitchen table conversations.

This book is also dedicated to all the people who have contributed case studies, tried the exercises in this book before going to press or been responsible for the proofreading. Thank you for sharing your views, experiences and questions to help make this book possible.

Self-confidence is an essential skill and enables each of us to live a full and worthwhile life. Thank you to everyone who has played a part in bringing this book to life and helping to make a difference to other people's lives.

About the Author:

Elizabeth lives in a village in the heart of the Cotswolds. Her home (a barn conversion) is the ideal space for creative thinking. It's also a place where friends and clients can step off the treadmill for a while and find themselves.

Elizabeth had a long and varied corporate career – including training, mentoring, quality auditing and key account management. Then in 2003 opportunity knocked on her door in the form of voluntary redundancy.

2003 – the year Dynamic Customer Solutions Ltd was born. This was a boutique consultancy specialising in personal development and improving the customer experience (win/win for everyone). Since then Elizabeth has worked with thousands of people from a wide range of backgrounds. This includes personal clients, start-ups, solopreneurs, the British Army, Chartered Institute of Housing, WH Smith and many of the UK's social housing providers.

In 2013 Elizabeth launched Shepherd Creative Learning as a tribute to Dennis Shepherd – who passed away unexpectedly in 2012. Dennis was the man who squared Elizabeth's circle personally and professionally, and encouraged her to utilise her skills as a writer and holistic therapist.

"It wasn't until my life fell apart following Dennis' death that I realised the importance of self-confidence. I've learnt that it's not possible to confront a major life change and continue to be your old self.

This very challenging period did wonders for my self-confidence, and now I'm paying it forward. I'm using my personal and career experience to help others be their most confident and fulfilled self".

Elizabeth writes her books based on her professional and personal experiences and knowledge. She believes passionately in the benefits of sharing skills and knowledge to help others create their own success stories.

"It's a privilege to provide support and encouragement to my clients. It's a humbling experience to watch clients break out of their restrictive cocoon and blossom into beautiful butterflies. My mum gave me the wings to fly; now that's what I'm doing for others".

If you would like to know more about Elizabeth or get in touch, you will find her on LinkedIn, Twitter and Facebook. LinkedIn profile (liz-tucker/10/531/68/), (Twitter - @liztucker03) and (Facebook https://www.facebook.com/shepherdcreativelearning1/). Alternatively, you can get in touch by email - shepherdcreativelearning@gmail.com

Table of Contents

Preface:

Self-confidence – of course you can survive without it but you'll only be living half the life you could have. Self-confidence gives you the courage to try new things and live life to the full.

Self-confidence is available to all of us; it's not an impossible dream. What's more, self-confidence doesn't recognise status, race, financial wealth or anything else that we use to define ourselves. Does that inspire you to reach out to self-confidence? I hope so!

I believe self-confidence makes each of us a nicer person as we don't feel threatened by others or constantly feel the need to prove our worth to everyone around us. Wouldn't it be lovely if everyone could demonstrate self-confidence all the time. Of course this isn't going to happen for a multitude of reasons.

Some don't have the desire or motivation to embrace self-confidence. Others may not have the support network or the funds to pay for professional help. Some may even believe it's not an option available to them.

Obviously professional help and support will help ensure you get the desired result. However, not everyone wants or can afford this option. The good news is you can still achieve your desired self-confidence level without professional help as long as you're willing to work at it.

Please know that doing nothing will fix nothing. This really is not a good choice for your long-term wellbeing. I hope A Matter of Self-confidence - Part II will help you in some small way. Trust me – there's an exciting world of opportunities waiting for you when you have the confidence to dip you toe in the water.

'A Matter of Self-confidence - Part II' is an easy to read and practical self-help book. Within these pages you will find a combination of subject matter, exercises, inspirational quotes and real-life case studies.

My aim in writing this book is to help you regain some of the faith in yourself that you've lost or never had. I'm not suggesting 'A Matter of Self-confidence' will fix all your self-confidence issues. However, it is designed to help you on your journey to a new, more confident you. As your self-confidence grows I'm sure you'll be motivated to keep going.

There are lots of books available on transactional analysis, neuro linguistic programming (NLP) and psychology, which include self-confidence. Most of these books are written from a technical or clinical perspective. A Matter of Self-confidence - Part II is written from a different professional perspective.

'A Matter of Self-confidence' is written from the perspective of an intuitive life coach. It's based on my personal experiences and the experiences of some of my clients. We've all chosen to share our knowledge and experience as we hope it will help you to become the most confident version of you possible. If you would like to share your story for future use please get in touch. Choose from: shepherdcreativelearning@gmail.com or http://www.shepherdcreativelearning.co.uk.

Some clients come to me as they need more confidence to achieve their professional goals. For some it was personal. The common thread running through everyone's journey is a desire for greater self-confidence. Without self-confidence you will always create boundaries that stop you achieving your full potential. Greater self-confidence really is one of the best gifts you can ever give yourself.

Like everyone else, I've had my share of confidence ups and downs. I've chosen to fight back and win. The thing is I have some idea of what you're going through. In short, I've walked the walk! This is not a theoretical book; it's a practical one based on real life experiences.

My lightbulb moment was when I realised that waiting for someone else's permission to be confident was a waste of my life. I've never looked back since I got this kick in the pants. Of course not every experience is positive but self-confidence helps me to take the rough with the smooth.

At the end of 2013 something magical happened – I had an idea to write a self-help book on self-confidence. It was another of those lightbulb moments. I was going through a horrible and life changing experience at the time but my self-confidence was steadily growing.

I also realised much of my time was spent helping clients improve their self-confidence. In the spring of 2014 'A Matter of Self-confidence' was born and started to grow organically. From this point onwards I started to pull together my skills, knowledge, experience and observations. I then asked some of my clients if I could share their personal stories too.

In 2015 I published the first version of 'A Matter of Self-confidence - (Parts I and II)'. Here we are in 2016 - 'A Matter of Self-confidence - (Parts I and II)' have now been helping people for over 12 months. Some report greater changes than others, but everyone has told me that they have benefitted in some way. I hope this small investment will open the door to new self-confidence and new opportunities for you too.

Trust me - everyone can increase their self-confidence but not everyone knows how to achieve it. That's my job! If you don't know how to achieve your desired level of self-confidence, find the help you need. This could be a professional life coach, home study programme, self-help book like this one, blog posts or your own support network. There are lots of options available. Doing nothing is the only option you should avoid.

Self-confidence is one of the best gifts you can ever give yourself. You won't regret it.

"A life without self-confidence is only half the life you could be living. Don't waste another day procrastinating" - Elizabeth J Tucker

1. Introduction

"Self-confidence is contagious" - Stephen Richards

Dealing with your self-confidence issues can be challenging, uncomfortable or even painful. It requires a great deal of soul searching and honesty. Only when you're willing to be totally honest with yourself will you really conquer your lack of self-confidence.

Now may or may not be the right time for you to overcome your self-limiting beliefs. You will only know the answer by asking "Am I ready to face to some painful memories or truths about myself".

If the answer is no, don't beat yourself up. Know that you can come back to this another time. If the answer is yes; well done you've taken the first step towards a new more confident you. Give yourself a virtual pat on the back.

In 'A Matter of Self-confidence - Part I' we explored the reasons for your lack of self-confidence. It was also an opportunity to put the foundations in place for a more confident future. 'A Matter of Self-confidence - Part II' is the fun bit.

Often my clients say "my goal is to increase my self-confidence". This is fine as a starting point, but this is not enough. The questions that immediately spring to mind are:

- In which areas of your life do you have self-confidence issues?
- What does self-confidence look like to you?
- When do you want to achieve this goal? A goal without a target date is pretty meaningless
- How are you going to achieve this goal?
- When are you going to start?
- What's your first step?
- What happens if you encounter setbacks?

It's important to recognise that knowing what you want and achieving it are very different things. I'm not saying this to put you off trying. I'm on your side and absolutely believe in your success.

You can be the confident person you dream of being, but are you willing to work at it? As with any goal, achievement comes from embracing change and focusing on the end result. If you put in the effort I guarantee you will be richly rewarded.

One way to improve your self-confidence is practice. View your self-confidence as a muscle that needs a regular workout. Do things that make you feel confident and do them often. Start with the easy stuff and work your way up to the big stuff. If this feels too scary, start with something you're already good at and get better at it, then move on to new activities.

Before moving on make a list of five actions you can take to recharge your self-confidence batteries. For example - remind yourself of all the things you're good at:

1.

2.

3.

4.

5.

Pick one action from your list and do it today. Already your journey to a new, more confident, you has begun. Not every step will be this easy, but self-confidence is available if you really want it.

Now there's a question - how much do you want self-confidence? On a scale of zero (no commitment) to ten (100% committed) how committed are you to achieving this goal? Be honest with yourself. If you're sufficiently committed you will get the desired result.

In order to recognise how much your self-confidence is growing you need to know what your starting point is.

Exercise: My Current Confidence Level

Thinking about your life, how confident are you currently?

1. Look at the chart below and put a cross in the place that represents your current self-confidence level. 0 = no confidence and 10 = very confident (not cocky or arrogant, just confident). Don't dwell on it; just place the cross where you instinctively feel is the right place

```
┌─────────────────────────────────────────────────────────┐
│                                                           │
│                                                           │
└─────────────────────────────────────────────────────────┘
```
   0   1   2   3   4   5   6   7   8   9   10

2. Wherever you have placed your cross (e.g. 4) imagine how you would feel if your score moved up just one place (e.g. 4 - 5). What would be different? How would this progress make you feel?

3. What is your desired confidence level? Make a note of this so you can see how close you get to your target score when you've finished the exercises in this book

"If you want to succeed you need to have the self-confidence and a strong conviction to know that you can" - Elizabeth J Tucker

Like any emotion, self-confidence ebbs and flows. As your self-confidence grows it will have a bigger part to play in your life. The challenges may also get bigger, but that's because you've learnt to overcome your fear of change, failure or success. Self-confidence will give you the skills and strength to overcome whatever challenges life throws at you.

Maintaining high levels of self-confidence and self-esteem are just as important as a healthy body. This is done through thoughtful and consistent action. Any time your self-confidence takes a dip think about your five actions for recharging your self-confidence batteries. Choose one from your list and off you go again.

Note: you might like to put your five actions for recharging your confidence batteries somewhere visible. This could be on the fridge door, near your computer, or anywhere else that feels right for you.

Are you ready to embark on your self-confidence journey? Or, do you have some emotional baggage you need to get rid of before you can make significant progress? The Letting Go Exercise might provide you with a launch pad for the new more confident you.

Exercise: The Letting Go Exercise

You may have been suppressing negative feelings and emotions for many years. That's not to say that you think about them regularly, but these are thoughts that are still in your mind. As long as negative thoughts remain in your consciousness they will create emotional clutter.

Are you ready to let go of the emotional clutter that is helping to stifle your self-confidence?

1. Get a piece of paper and some blue or pink ink (the colour of the ink is important. Blue is the colour of communication and pink represents love)

2. Think of an experience that caused you a crisis of confidence? This experience can be from any time in your life. Write this experience or situation in as much detail as you can remember

3. You can write this as an account of what happened or as a letter to the person who caused your pain. Note: if you're writing a letter, you're not going to send it to anyone

4. Allow all your suppressed feelings to come to the surface. Release all bitterness, resentment and past grievances. You may even have some happy memories or positive comments you want to include

5. Write every thought down. This could take anything from a few minutes to several days to complete. Don't put yourself under pressure; just work at the pace that feels right for you

6. When you've finished writing put your document or letter somewhere safe for a couple of days. Don't look at it during this time

7. When you feel ready read your document one last time. Tell yourself it's time to let go of this negative memory

8. Are you ready to release this memory? If so, light a candle and hold the paper over the flame. Allow the paper to burn completely

9. As the paper burns visualise yourself letting go of this experience or memory. Know this negative memory no longer serves a purpose in your life

10. Finally, complete the emotional healing process by saying "I forgive you and release you"

11. If this memory ever pops back into your mind again, know that you will feel no emotional attachment to it. This memory can no longer affect your self-confidence. It will just be a fleeting memory

You can do this exercise any time you identify some emotional clutter that needs shifting. Be kind to yourself - sometimes it will be easier than other times.

Self-confidence is a mental state that requires clear thinking. Trying to operate at 90 miles an hour with your mind racing with chatter is not a recipe for success. Now is a great time to learn to relax. The more relaxed you feel the more creative your brain will be. The more relaxed, creative and happy you are the more confident you will feel.

Develop a self-confidence ritual that you can go through whenever your confidence dips. Whatever strategy you opt for the important thing is to implement it whenever you need it. Even the most confident people experience a dip on occasions.

When you're feeling low, allow yourself a brief period of self-pity or woe is me. Don't allow this negative thinking to take hold though. Set a limit on how long you're going to allow this negativity; then pick yourself up and move forward again.

If one of your self-confidence issues is walking into a meeting or a party be the first to arrive. You will instantly feel more confident as you know you haven't got to walk into a room full of people. Little steps eventually lead to greater self-confidence.

Being surrounded by people who demonstrate genuine self-confidence will increase your own self-confidence. If you're thinking these people will make you feel worse then you're rubbing shoulders with the wrong people.

The people who make your feel worse are arrogant or superficially confident. Genuine and sincerely confident people will never make you feel inferior. They don't need to make anyone feel bad as they are already comfortable in their own skin.

It's no good simply observing the tactics of confident people. In order for you to develop self-confidence you need to experiment with different strategies. This requires a willingness to change. Often people who lack self-confidence are in a comfortable rut. Of course most would deny this. Did you find yourself denying it when you read the statement?

Don't wait until you're in a pressurised situation before you start experimenting with self-confidence strategies. This will simply add to your issues. Instead start by practicing some self-confidence strategies in stages and safe environments. Remember, self-confidence wants to be your friend, but like all friendships it needs some nurturing.

"When you have confidence, you can have a lot of fun. And when you have fun, you can do amazing things" - Joe Namath

2. Reasons To Be Confident

"If you have self-confidence whatever you want to try the future is open to you" - Elizabeth J Tucker

Who doesn't want to be confident? I can't think of anyone who really wants to spend their entire life battling a lack of self-confidence. It's hard work and exhausting.

True self-confidence comes from your life experiences, overcoming obstacles and learning new skills. Don't fall into the trap of craving self-confidence so much that you create a fear of failure. This will simply create self-limiting beliefs that will hold you back.

Fear is such a great inhibitor. It has the power to stop you achieving your full potential, or even just fully enjoying your life. If you can overcome your fears you will be happier, healthier, more positive and probably a lot more successful. Don't get into a comfortable rut in your state of fear. Instead, face your fear of being confident.

Exercise: My Fear of Being Confident

This exercise has been deliberately designed to be short to quickly dispel any fears you may have of being confident. You will need a piece of paper and a pen for this exercise.

1. Write a list of all your fears of being confident. For example, fear of failure or how confidence might change you, losing some of the people close to you etc. These may be real or imagined fears

2. What can you do to overcome these fears? For example, find a confidence buddy or create your own reward and penalty system etc

3. Is there any real basis for your fears? Sometimes there is and sometimes there isn't

4. Try to remember a time in your life when you felt so confident that other people's opinions didn't matter? Visualise this situation as clearly as possible. Now fix this in your memory

5. Whenever your confidence dips recall your memory from step 4. Try to recapture the experience in your mind. If may only provide a short-term self-confidence boost but often this is enough

---

I'm not suggesting quick fixes will provide long-term solutions. However, even the longest journey starts with a single step. Every quick fix or step you take towards self-confidence has a key role in helping you achieve your goal.

Self-confidence is good for you and everyone you meet. A win/win outcome. Are you still wondering why would you want to be confident? There are many reasons why self-confidence is a good thing. Here are just a few to get you thinking:

- Self-confidence teaches you to appreciate and value yourself
- Confident people are easier to talk to and be with
- Confident people are like a human magnet. Others are naturally drawn to you if you exude self-confidence
- Confident people are easier to get to know. The more someone knows about you the greater the chance they will offer you new opportunities or friendship
- Confident people believe in their own skills, talents and abilities. They don't rely on others to tell them
- Confident people are more likely to take risks or try new things. Even if they don't know if they will succeed, they are more likely to try
- Confident people find it easier to overcome setbacks. They are more likely to dust themselves off when things go wrong and then carry on. People who lack self-confidence often waste time beating themselves up
- Self-confidence often gives people clarity around their values
- Self-confidence gives you a tremendous sense of achievement, which sits deep inside you. Any time you're having a blip you can recall an achievement that gave you a sense of increased self-confidence. It's a great quick fix
- Self-confidence develops a strong self-belief system
- Confident people aren't reliant on other people to make them feel good
- Confident people aren't unduly concerned about the opinions of other people. They have a balanced approach to their own and other people's opinions
- Genuine self-confidence creates humility
- Confident people have a heightened self-awareness
- Self-confidence often creates credibility

- Confident people are better at self-acceptance
- Self-confidence helps you develop excellent interpersonal skills

Being confident has many benefits, and not just in your personal life. Self-confidence is beneficial in your professional life and your business. Whatever your ambitions, building your self-confidence will play a key role in helping you achieve success.

Are you genuinely committed to being confident, or is it just a nice to have? If you want self-confidence you can achieve it. Success is guaranteed if you put in the effort. What isn't guaranteed is the level of self-confidence you will achieve. This will be down to you.

Assuming you do want to be confident, my questions to you are why? What are the benefits to you personally of developing self-confidence?

Exercise: Reasons To Be Confident

Don't spend too long doing a deep self-analysis. Just write down whatever thoughts come into your head. I just want to get self-confidence back onto your radar as it may have been missing for a long time.

1. Spend no more than 15 minutes answering this question - "What are my top 10 reasons for wanting to develop self-confidence?" I've written the first one to get you started, but you can change this is you wish

a. I will feel much better about myself

b.

c.

d.

e.

f.

g.

h.

i.

j.

2. If you didn't come up with 10 reasons don't worry about it. You can always try this exercise again another time. The aim of the exercise was to get you wanting self-confidence

3. On a scale of 0 (none) - 10 (failure is not an option) what is your commitment level? Spend a few minutes thinking about your commitment level. I know I asked this question in Chapter 1, but this is a question that you really should ask yourself regularly. It's easy to become bored or defeated if you don't have something to motivate you

If you have the self-confidence to believe in yourself more opportunities are likely to appear for you. Self-confidence means you will perform better; even if you don't know how initially. If you try something and it doesn't work, dust yourself off and try again or move on.

Unfortunately, if you lack self-confidence you're more likely to use it as a stick to beat yourself with. This is a very unhelpful behaviour. The sooner you can break this cycle the sooner your self-confidence will be able to develop.

So, my challenge to you is be on the lookout for opportunities. When an opportunity presents itself, make a note of what it is in your diary or journal. Also note what action you took; even if you turned it down. The important thing is you spotted the opportunity.

As your self-confidence grows you will notice that you seize more and more opportunities, rather than rejecting them. This is a sure-fire sign your self-confidence is on the increase. Self-confidence will also give you the skills to face crises that come your way as you travel on the path to success.

If you're going to develop lasting self-confidence then you need to accept that this comes with uncertainty. Furthermore, you will experience some setbacks on your journey. Don't let this stop you progressing.

Have I managed to convince you that self-confidence has lots to offer you? I do hope so.

Ask yourself what you would do if you were immune to other people's opinions and criticism. This might be a good time to indulge your imagination. Imagine yourself as truly confident and have a go at this short exercise. You will need a piece of paper and a pen for this exercise.

Exercise: Imagine Yourself As Confident

We've all read stories where your Fairy Godmother grants a single wish. Imagine your Fairy Godmother could make it possible for you to be totally confident for an entire day. Imagine she's able to let you experience anything you wish on this day. She wants you to understand what difference self-confidence will make to your life.

1. For the first part of this exercise all you need is your imagination. Allow your mind a free rein to be at its creative best

2. Imagine today you have no self-confidence issues at all. Today you are just brimming with self-confidence. When you're ready answer the following questions:

a. How are you walking around (e.g. upright or slouched, striding or small regular steps)?

b. How do you sound? Does your voice sound different to normal?

c. How do you feel inside? Sense all the feelings you experience on this day of complete self-confidence

d. Is it easier to talk to strangers today because you have no self-confidence issues?

e. What changes are your family and friends seeing in you?

f. Are you behaving differently at work? If yes, what is different?

g. Are people treating you differently? If so, how are they treating you?

h. Are you treating others differently? If yes, what is different?

3. Once you answered all the questions spend a few minutes reflecting on your thoughts

4. Ask yourself "Would I be happier as the new me?" If so, surely it's a goal worth working towards. You don't have to stay trapped in a cycle of little or no self-confidence unless you want to

5. Name one minor change you're willing to make as the first step on the journey to a new more confident you. Remember, even the longest journey begins with a single step

6. Write this change down. Write it in as much detail as possible as this will help to keep you motivated

7. Set a target date for achieving this minor change. Before you go any further decide what your reward will be

8. When you've made this minor change reward your success in some way

Note: You can use this exercise for any self-confidence goal you choose to set yourself. Small steady steps are generally easier to achieve than a massive leap.

Deciding that you want to be confident is great, but it's only the start. The important part is the action you take to develop your self-confidence.

The difference between those who succeed and those who don't is commitment. You've probably heard the expression 'winners never quit and quitters never win'. This absolutely applies to self-confidence. It takes time and effort to develop self-confidence but the rewards make it worthwhile.

Lack of self-confidence will stop you achieving your goals. Self-confidence, on the other hand, will enable you to achieve even things that seem impossible. Here's my personal story about digging deep and finding the self-confidence to learn to swim as an adult.

To you it may seem like nothing, but at the time I felt like I had a mountain to climb.

Case Study: Overcoming fear and finding a new self-confidence

Due to lack of self-confidence and a fear of the water, I didn't learn to swim until 2008. I had tried on many occasions to learn to swim, but up until this point each attempt had failed. This time was going to be different as I had a strong motivation to succeed.

My mum had never learnt to swim, and always regretted it. When my mum died in 2008 I decided that 'no matter what' I was going to learn to swim for her. I wanted to make my mum proud of me, and I wanted to achieve something special for her. Even though my mum's no longer here I'm sure she would be proud of my achievement.

Learning to swim was a painful, challenging and incredibly frustrating experience for me and my swimming instructor. I even had several hypnotherapy sessions to help me overcome my fear; such was my determination to succeed this time. On many occasions I wanted to give up, but I was doing this for my mum. I couldn't let her down.

I slugged away at my swimming lessons every week for several months. Most weeks I hated it, if I'm honest. Eventually I could swim; just a few metres but I could swim. Then I could swim 25 metres and got a certificate. I kept slugging away until I had the self-confidence and ability to swim two lengths of the pool. I was so proud of myself.

Newly found self-confidence is very fragile and should be treated with the utmost care! My swimming instructor obviously missed this point. After I was able to swim two lengths of the pool fairly happily my swimming instructor upped the stakes. She decided it was time for me to swim and float on my back.

I really didn't want to do this, but she absolutely insisted. We had several aborted attempts at this, but with each attempt I became more agitated and upset. Still my swimming instructor pressed on; she was determined that I was going to do this. On one occasion my panic was so severe I almost drowned. I got out of the pool and didn't get back into a swimming pool until 2011.

My self-confidence had been shattered and now I was back to square one. In 2011 Dennis and I went to Crete for a holiday. He eventually persuaded me to get back into the swimming pool with him.

I didn't have the self-confidence to move away from the edge of the pool or swim at first. At least I was in the pool, which was an achievement. Dennis spent hours every day of that holiday coaxing and encouraging me to swim. He was unbelievably patient, which anyone who knew Dennis would confirm wasn't his natural way.

Dennis' patience paid off; eventually I started to swim again. Thanks to Dennis, I came back from Crete swimming again. I'm never going to be a natural water baby, but thanks to Dennis I now have the self-confidence to get in the pool and swim.

I'm not a great swimmer, and I don't swim regularly. The important thing is I can now swim. What's more I've been told by other swimmers (including two swimming instructors) that I have a good style.

My mum gave me the motivation to succeed. This kept me going when I wanted to give up. Dennis knew how important this was to me. He gave me all the time I needed to overcome my irrational fear of swimming for a second time.

This experience taught me that overcoming my fears gave me new self-confidence. It's also taught me that self-confidence is fragile initially and must be nurtured. Nowadays I decide when to push myself and when to be gentle with myself.

Without these two incredible human beings I wouldn't be swimming now. My advice to you is, if you have a big goal find someone to support you. It will make a tremendous difference.

Liz (Overcoming fear and finding new confidence author)

Have I convinced you that self-confidence is a goal worth achieving? Self-confidence sits deep inside you. You can tap into it anytime you need a little boost. Personally, I believe self-confidence is a goal worth working towards.

"Go confidently in the direction of your dreams and live the life you have imagined" - Henry David Thoreau

3. Common Features Of Self-confidence

"Self-confidence comes from experience. Therefore, experience as much as you possibly can" - Elizabeth J Tucker

What is self-confidence? What does it look like, and how do we describe it to others? In reality, it means something different to each of us. What one person sees as self-confidence another may perceive to be arrogance.

The dictionary definition of self-confidence is 'belief in oneself and one's powers or abilities'.

True self-confidence is a good thing. It's a positive mental state that will make you feel good. This may be a 'can do' attitude, a sense of calm and peace or you may feel energised.

Self-confidence is a genuine self-appreciation. It's rather like viewing yourself as an objective observer would and liking what you see. I'm sure you look at family, friends and colleagues in this way, so do the same thing for yourself.

As human beings we seem to be programmed to be modest. Most of us aren't naturally comfortable saying we're good at something. No wonder we have self-confidence issues. What a shame to bury your abilities and not give them the recognition they deserve.

Every piece of knowledge or skill has been earnt. Every experience has involved change and maybe even discomfort. Each one has contributed to your self-confidence. Give yourself the recognition you deserve.

The power to be confident resides inside you, not someone else. Imagine all the potential opportunities available to you if you allow yourself to be confident. Self-confidence comes from embracing who you are, not beating yourself up about your imperfections. Genuine self-confidence is not superficial bravado. It's a self-esteem that will get you through the good times and bad.

How do you decide someone is confident? Is it a calm self-assurance, an assertive manner or an air of boldness? Everyone has their own answer to the question 'what is self-confidence'? Don't be fooled into thinking the most talkative person is the most confident.

Exercise: My Idea of Self-confidence

Self-confidence looks, sounds and feels different to each of us. That's because we're unique and no two people will have identical views or experiences. When you're looking at other people how do you decide whether they are confident or not?

Food for thought maybe!

1. Consider this, how do you decide whether someone else is confident or not? You can focus on your family, friends or colleagues for this exercise. You may observe a famous person on the television or it could be a stranger. Just spend a few moments pondering this question

2. When you're ready write 10 things that tell you that someone is confident

a.

b.

c.

d.

e.

f.

g.

h.

i.

j.

3. Don't get too bogged down with this. If after 10 minutes you're struggling to answer the question, leave it. You may need to come back to this another time. The chances are you've never consciously thought about this before

4. Now consider what you've written for a moment. How do you know the person you were thinking about is confident? What evidence do you have?

It's all a matter of perception. Your perception is this person is confident, but you really don't know this to be the case. It could simply be a public persona. None of us really knows what goes on in someone else's headspace.

Have you ever taken the time to get to know or closely observe successful people? Have you noticed that outwardly they appear very confident? Imagine Sir Richard Branson, Hilary Clinton, The Dalai Lama or Oprah Winfrey. I don't know any of these people, but each has been successful in their chosen field. What's more, each of them seems to exude self-confidence in their own way.

Of course self-confidence may have come to them as a result of their success. Usually it's the other way around though. Like everyone else they will have had some self-limiting beliefs on the way. They had the self-confidence to step outside their comfort zone, overcome their self-limiting beliefs and stretch themselves. The result of this was success, but it almost certainly increased their self-confidence too.

Whether you are confident or lack of self-confidence there are some common features. In 'A Matter of Self-confidence - Part I' I included a chapter on the common traits of lack of self-confidence. Now let's look at some of the common features of self-confidence.

Here's some good news about self-confidence that you may not have considered. Self-confidence is contagious; it's free and available to everyone. Knowing this, wouldn't you want it? Here are some common features of self-confidence; consider which ones apply to you:

- An easy-going attitude. This doesn't mean so laid back you're almost asleep
- Handling different opinions, pressures and attitudes with grace and giving the impression of being comfortable in your own skin
- Not obsessing over what other people think of you
- Neither needy, clingy or always trying to be the centre of attention
- Assertively sending out the message "I'm the leader of my own life"
- Caring enough about yourself to develop a positive, healthy self-image
- Communicating who you are on the inside as well as the outside
- Being aware of what you say and do so you never come across as being 'above' anyone else
- Having a sense of humour. Being able to enjoy humour in all its guises; including an ability to laugh at yourself
- Making it easy for others to be with or around you
- Quick to give praise and recognition to others. This builds the other persons self-confidence too

- Standing up for what you believe in. Placing your values and beliefs above being liked
- Seizing every opportunity to genuinely smile. This radiates sparkle and enthusiasm, which is contagious
- Feeling comfortable making eye contact (not staring though)
- Accepting or even embracing change
- Being proud of your achievements and graciously accepting the recognition
- Accepting personal responsibility for your decisions and actions
- Acting in spite of your fears and reservations, not because of them
- Setting and achieving your goals to realise your dreams
- Recognise that it's human to make mistakes and so taking it in your stride
- Accepting criticism in the spirit it is intended and not automatically assuming it's a personal attack
- Recognising that on occasions you will face difficult or challenging situations, but not expecting the worse before it's happened
- An ability to not over analyse things

This list is not exhaustive, but hopefully it's helped you want to increase your own self-confidence. How many of these self-confidence traits did you recognise in yourself? Review this list and tick each trait that you recognise in you. Don't be too modest.

When you surround yourself with genuinely confident people it will increase your self-confidence too. Next time you're with confident people notice how their positivity rubs off on you. It may only be a minor change, but you will feel different inside.

Equally, when you're radiating self-confidence you will have a positive impact on others. You may be unaware of the influence you're having but it will be happening anyway. Start to notice how people react differently to you when you're glowing with self-confidence.

Self-confidence will give you the courage to set goals for yourself, and expect to achieve success. Of course there's always a risk of failure. If you feel confident your chance of success is greater and failure doesn't matter so much.

Never view failure as a bad thing. It's simply a message to you saying 'try it another way'. If you give up every time something doesn't work out exactly as you wanted, first time around, you'll never develop self-confidence.

Self-confidence is an essential ingredient in any competitive environment e.g. sport or business. Self-confidence also has a key role to play in your personal life.

Self-confidence will enable you to take risks and push yourself outside your comfort zone. It will enable you to make the most of every aspect of your life. Finally, self-confidence will help you to be assertive, rather than passive or aggressive. You will find more about assertive, passive and aggressive behaviour in chapter 5 - Communication and self-confidence.

Learn to accept and genuinely like who you are. This is absolutely fundamental to developing sustainable self-confidence. Lack of self-confidence often comes from trying to be someone you're not. Do yourself a favour and embrace the lovely person you are.

What does your self-confidence look, sound and feel like to you? It's important to know how you personally feel and demonstrate self-confidence. If you can't define this how will you know when you've achieved the level of self-confidence you're seeking? Here's a short exercise to help answer this question.

Exercise: What I Experience When I Feel Confident or Lack Self-confidence

Like every other internal experience the way you feel when you're feeling confident or lacking self-confidence is unique to you. This quick exercise is an opportunity to reflect on what you experience when you're feeling confident or lacking in self-confidence.

This exercise should take you less than 15 minutes. All you need is a piece of paper and a pen.

1. On your piece of paper create two columns. The headings are 'Feeling Confident' and 'Lack of Self-confidence'

2. Ask yourself the following question "how do I feel when I'm confident?" Don't think too hard; just allow the thoughts to drift into your mind. Write whatever thoughts come into your head. Typical answers include - happy,

relaxed, capable and valued etc. Spend no more than 3-4 minutes on this question

3. Now ask yourself the following question - 'How do I feel when I lack self-confidence?' Write whatever thoughts come into your head. For example, anxious, dry mouth, butterflies etc. Spend no more than 3-4 minutes on this question

4. Ignore the answers to questions 2 and 3 for a moment. Think of a time when you did something well and felt pleased with yourself. Write down the details of this event

5. Now think of a time when you failed at something. Write your memory of this down too

6. Now look at your lists from questions 2 and 3. Which list has most entries? If your 'Feeling Confident' list has more entries, increasing your self-confidence will be an easier task for you

7. Thinking about questions 4 and 5, which example was easiest to remember? Were your memories more vivid for this event?

8. Finally, do you normally find it easier to remember positive feelings and experiences, or negative feelings and experiences?

9. Your answer to question 8 will indicate whether your natural default position is positive or negative. Confident people generally have a 'positive' default position. If your default position is negative, make a pledge to counteract every negative thought with a positive one in future. Or, at least try to do this

Most people recollect negative experiences more strongly than positive ones. Does this describe you? If so, this thinking helps reinforce your lack of self-confidence. We all have a mixture of positive and negative experiences. The key to success is giving the positive ones more headspace.

It's important to learn from your mistakes and negative experiences. However, don't allow the little voice inside you make you feel bad. Whatever the negative experience it's not the end of the world. Follow the example of your more confident friends and colleagues. Confident people pick themselves up, dust themselves off and move forward.

If you dwell on mistakes or negative experiences it will make you nervous. The more nervous you become the less confident you will feel. The less confident you feel the less likely you are to try new things. This simply creates a repetitive negative cycle. It's important to break this cycle and replace self-criticism with encouragement and self-praise.

"For each of us 'the devil' is something different. It could be self-confidence, stress or anything else. Whatever it is - don't let the devil through the door" - Elizabeth J Tucker

Some days and some situations are easier than others, but that's life. Of course lack of self- confidence can creep up on you at any time. Instead of focusing on this, focus on the qualities that are most apparent when you feel confident.

Self-confidence doesn't recognise colour, sex, religion or anything else. As I've said before, self-confidence is available to anyone who welcomes it. I agree that it's harder for some people to achieve self-confidence than others, but it's not impossible. Are you ready to welcome self-confidence into your life?

The way in which we develop self-confidence is different for all of us. Improving your observation skills can help when developing your self-confidence. As babies and toddlers we learnt many of our skills by observing others. Why not try observing confident people and adopting some of their habits. The chances are this is what they did in the initial stages of self-confidence building.

Next time you're at an event with several other people observe them walking into the room. This can be a business meeting, social event or anything else. You could even try observing people in a train station or airport. The confident ones will stand out from the others.

This short exercise is designed to test your observation skills.

Exercise: Notice How Confident People Walk Into a Room

Most people are unaware of being observed when they walk into a room so they don't put on a performance. You will notice the confident ones share common traits. Some things to look out for are - posture, eye contact, facial expressions and body language.

1. When you're ready start observing

2. The first thing to do is pay attention to everyone's posture. Notice whether people hold their head high or look down at the floor. Confident people generally keep their head up, spine straight and shoulders down

3. Next, observe the eye contact. Confident people will scan the room as they enter, whereas those lacking in self-confidence will keep their eyes down or avoid eye contact if possible

4. Now notice the facial expressions. The more confident people feel the less tense their facial muscles will be

5. Notice the pace as people walk into the room. Confident people never reluctantly shuffle into a room. Often they either stride into a room or casually stroll in. Either way, they appear comfortable in their own skin

6. Notice how people sit or stand. You rarely see confident people slouching

7. Now observe how easily the confident ones interact and communicate with others

8. Once you've finished observing, spend a few minutes reflecting on what you noticed. This should be a combination of confident and non-confident behaviours

9. Thinking about the observations you made, identify which confidence traits you already demonstrate

10. Now consider your non-confident traits. Make a mental note to deal with these

As you become more accomplished at this exercise you will be able to fine tune your observations skills. Then you can start to look for signs of tension around the eyes and jawline. These aren't immediately obvious signs like the others, but on close observation you will notice them.

If you start practicing this observation exercise regularly it will become second nature to you. Once this becomes firmly fixed in your mind the chances are you will subconsciously start mirroring some of their behaviours. That's the power of subliminal messaging. It's rather like having a mentor, only they won't know they are mentoring you.

Confident people seem to fill the space when they enter the room. They seem to have a presence even if they aren't doing anything. This presence has nothing to do with their clothes or physique; it's something from within.

Before we move on from the common features of self-confidence here's quick summary of some common behaviours that suggest self-confidence:

- Doing what you believe to be right, even if others mock or criticise you for it
- Being willing to take risks and go the extra mile to achieve greater things
- Admitting and accepting your mistakes, and then learning from them
- Accepting compliments graciously
- Not needing others to congratulate you as you're comfortable with your own abilities. Praise is just a 'nice to have'

The next list comprises common behaviours that suggest a lack of self-confidence:

- Doing what other people think or expect of you
- Staying in your comfort zone, fearing failure, and so avoiding taking risks
- Working hard to cover up your mistakes and hoping that you can fix the problem before anyone notices
- Dismissing compliments offhandedly. You know this is due to your lack of self-confidence but others often treat it as a rejection of their attempts to be sincere
- Waiting for others to congratulate you on your accomplishments

Which of these lists most closely describes you currently? Once you can identify the traits and behaviours of confident people you can start practicing them too.

In the initial stages of development, self-confidence needs all the help it can get. It's very fragile and vulnerable until it becomes established in your psyche. Be kind to yourself, and know that you will get there. Just keep the goal firmly fixed in your mind.

"Love yourself and respect others. This is the recipe for success and self-confidence" - Unknown

---

4. The Link Between Positive Thinking And Self-confidence

"You may not control all the events that happen to you, but you can decide not to be reduced by them" - Maya Angelou

Like many others, I believe there is a link between positive thinking, intuition and self-confidence. Let's start with positive thinking.

Over the last ten years there has been lots of research into the benefits of positive thinking. This research is still ongoing, and there are bound to be contradictory findings over time. However, for now the general conclusion seems to be that there is a link between positive thinking and self-confidence.

Aside from anything else, positive thinking makes you feel better. It's much easier to feel confident when you're in a positive state of mind. To me, this alone is a good reason to adopt positive thinking. The key to positive thinking is:

- Recognition - recognising that change is needed. The world around you is constantly evolving and you need to change too
- Self-interest - the motivation to change. This is all about being interested in your own personal development (new skills, emotional or spiritual). Personal development increases self-confidence
- Making changes - this includes your thoughts, actions, attitude and beliefs. Positive thinkers generally achieve better results
- Overcoming fear - doubt is the biggest opposition to positive thinking and achieving your goals. Your fears may be fear of change, failure or success. Don't let fear stop you being confident
- Self-nurturing - be gentle and loving with yourself. Just like everyone else, you need nurturing

Current research suggests that those with a 'solutions focused' approach to life are more productive, more influential and get better results. Research also suggests that those who focus on their problems seem to become ill more often. I know this sounds like a sweeping statement. Of course this won't apply to everyone, but it's worth considering none-the-less.

If you're prone to analysing your life make sure you give more attention to your successes than failures. I've found those clients who are prone to analysing their life give more attention to their failures. I'm not making a sweeping statement here; I'm just describing my experience with my own clients. Over analysing the things that go wrong will crush your self-confidence

By focusing on what you can do you're retraining your brain to notice positive situations. Get into the habit of focusing on feeling good about yourself and just accepting when things go wrong. This is a great way to develop self-confidence, and a more positive outlook. The added bonus is you will be much better company for the people around you.

You have thousands of thoughts every day. Your mind is an extraordinary instrument. It thinks, feels, imagines, decides, chooses, believes, dreams, remembers and analyses all the time. All of these processes can be done in a positive or negative way. The choice is yours. I challenge you to choose positive thinking.

Are you naturally a positive thinker? This visualisation exercise is an opportunity to practice positive thinking.

Exercise: Positive Thinking

Are you naturally positive? Consider your inner self as a library of positivity. By using your mind and thoughts in the right way, you can access your natural store of positive strength. It just takes a little effort. Are you up for the challenge? If so, try this visualisation exercise.

What are you thinking right now? Are your thoughts positive or negative?

1. What type of thoughts do you experience most often? Thoughts generally fall into the following categories:

a. Wasteful - thinking too much about things that you can't control. These thoughts are often linked to the past or the future

b. Negative - these thoughts are linked to negative/destructive feelings (e.g. sadness, anger, jealousy, anxiety etc). Negative thoughts are not beneficial to anyone

c. Neutral - necessary events, such as buying toothpaste or collecting your children from school. These thoughts are harmless unless they become obsessive

d. Positive - these thoughts are beneficial to you and others. You can train your mind to focus on positive thoughts. They will help you to feel emotionally lighter

2. Find somewhere quiet to sit for a few minutes. Stop what you're doing and simply observe your thoughts for approximately 3-5 minutes. Allow your thoughts to come and go for a few minutes. Don't make any judgements about these thoughts; just watch and see your attitude, perception and beliefs

3. Stop and take stock for a moment. How did you find the experience?

4. Now start again. For the next 3-5 minutes continue observing your thoughts. This time whatever thought pops into your mind, consider "is this thought beneficial to me?" If not, what would you like to be thinking instead?

5. Finally steer your thoughts in a positive way. Ask yourself "How do I want to feel right now? What thoughts do I need to have in order to create this feeling?" If you're struggling with this part of the exercise, read on…

a. Think of a feeling or quality that you would like to experience right now
b. What colour, symbols, words or scene reminds you of the feeling you want to achieve? If you chose peace as the answer to the previous question, what colour and words symbolise peace for you?

Visualise or write down all the words that come into your mind when you think of your chosen feeling or quality. Use a gentle tone as if you were talking to a small child. If any unwanted thoughts come into your mind replace them with positive thoughts

Here's an example of the exercise so you can follow what I'm saying:

a. I would like to feel peace right now
b. To me peace looks like a clear blue sky. Sky blue is soft and gentle; it's light, cool, soothing and calming, all at the same time. When I look at the sky I see white fluffy clouds gently moving across the sky. I imagine myself up there in the clouds and hear nothing but silence. I use this silence to still my mind and be peaceful for a few minutes

When you practice self-talk you become the ruler of your mind. At this point the power is created within your mind. You can now begin to develop the power of positivity.

If you want to make your mind your best friend create a positive conversation in your head as often as possible. Try talking to yourself in a positive way. Take a few minutes every day to do this. If you do this self-talk regularly you can make positive thinking your default. This will be good for your self-confidence and your overall sense of wellbeing.

Never underestimate the power of positive thinking. Yu may not always get exactly what you think you want, exactly when you want it. If you stay focused you will get what you want, or something better, at the right time.

I've been consciously practicing positive thinking for many years. As a result I'm in a happier and healthier place emotionally. I've included my own personal story about my own experience of the power of positive thinking.

Case Study: The power of positive thinking

Buying a house is probably the biggest purchase most of us make. If we're lucky we do it with someone else and share the responsibility. I'd done this several times, but in the mid-1990s I found myself in a position where I needed to go it alone.

As I was purchasing on my own this time my buying power was significantly reduced. If I'm honest most of what was available to me I didn't like. I needed to get over this as I didn't want to rent forever.

After three months of searching and endless viewings I found a place to call home. It was a small and modest 1930s semi-detached house. The old lady who owned the house had been taken into residential care and the house was empty.

This was to be a very simple and straightforward transaction as I was being treated as a first-time buyer, and there was no onward chain on the other party's side. Everything was going swimmingly and completion was well within my reach. Then everything changed.

On the day we were due to exchange contracts there were no family members available. This meant someone else would need to take the contract to the homeowner so she could sign it. Her solicitor opted to do this himself so the matter could be completed quickly.

At this point the solicitor discovered the homeowner was suffering from dementia. She had no idea what any of the documents were that she'd been signing. Suddenly everything ground to a halt. The matter needed to go to the Court of Protection before the property could be sold to me.

If you've ever had any dealings with the Court of Protection you will know this is a long and tiresome process. Matters seem to drag on endlessly in these cases before reaching a conclusion. Time wasn't on my side. My tenancy was coming to an end. Also, if I didn't complete within a certain timescale I would lose my relocation package from my employer. That focused my attention.

I wanted that little house and was absolutely determined I was going to have it. Not for one minute did I allow doubt to enter my mind. I just stayed focused and determined to win.

To cut a long story short, I got what I wanted and within the necessary timescale. In the process I alienated both solicitors and terrorised the estate agent. My own solicitor banned me from ever being a client of the firm again. He said I was a 'pain in the neck' and they didn't want me as a client again.

I spent 14 happy years in that little house. More importantly, by staying positive and focused I got what I wanted.

Positive thinking can achieve amazing results if you're willing to commit to your goal! I've proved this to myself many times since this incident.

(Liz - The power of positive thinking author)

We've all had the day when everything seems to go wrong. For example - you slept through the alarm and stubbed your toe while getting out of bed. Next you got stuck in a traffic jam and arrived late for work. When you got to work you found a pile of tasks, all requiring your immediate attention.

For most of us, our immediate thought is the Universe is working against me. Has it ever occurred to you that the Universe is equally capable of working in your favour? You don't need any tools to do this exercise as it's designed to be a visualisation exercise. However, you may prefer to write your memories down.

Exercise: The Universe Conspiring For or Against You

When was the last time you had a brilliant day and convinced yourself the Universe was conspiring in your favour? The chances are you have never done this. Let's see how good you are at remembering the good experiences.

1. Start by trawling through your memory bank to recall a time when everything seemed to conspire against you. Remember the scenario in as much detail as possible

2. Now visualise the opposite. Remember a day or situation where everything went really well or your day was filled with lots of lovely surprises

3. Do you believe the Universe was conspiring against you in scenario one? Do you believe the Universe was conspiring in your favour for scenario two?

4. Are both of your answers to question 3 yes or no? It's impossible to believe yes for one question and no for the other one. Logically, you can't believe that everything can go wrong for you if you don't believe everything can go well for you.

Whatever you focus most attention on is what you will manifest. So, if you spend all your time expecting negative outcomes that's exactly what you will get. If your time is spent focusing on positive outcomes that's what you will achieve. You may not always get exactly what you asked for but you will achieve positive outcomes none-the-less.

Once you recognise that your thoughts are drawing your experiences and outcomes to you then you have the power to harness positive thinking. If this feels like a step too far try counteracting every negative thought with a positive one. Once you've got the hang of this you can start consciously using positive thinking.

This positive thinking is known as pronoia (pronounced pro-noy-a). Whenever you need a confidence boost adopt a bit of pronoia. Developing an unwavering belief that the Universe is conspiring to help you is an effective way to increase your self-confidence.

On reading this you may be thinking pronoia is a load of rubbish. Fine, but you can't justify negative thinking if you don't believe in positive thinking. How can you believe that everything is conspiring against you if you don't believe things can conspire in your favour?

The Law of Attraction states that whatever you focus most attention on you manifest. Therefore, if you devote your life to the 'glass half empty' mindset you will always be aware of negative things first. This may result in you missing some golden opportunities.

I've been consciously using the Law of Attraction and pronoia for many years. This has given me a much more positive approach to life. I believe it's also increased my ability to spot opportunities when they're presented to me.

With a positive attitude, you can bounce back quicker. When life kicks you in the teeth it doesn't feel as bad as it would to someone with a negative default position. Positive thinking enables you to view negative experiences as life lessons. Dust yourself off, learn from the experience and then move on.

If you're still feeling some resistance to positive thinking, consider this... positive thinking is more likely to make you a people magnet. Most of us prefer to avoid negative people as their energy can pull us down. Life can be pretty lonely if people are always trying to avoid spending time with you.

I could provide you with lots of examples of people who view life positively. All report that they're experiencing better luck than during their previous negative mindset. However, I think you will feel the impact more if you find your own examples. Look the at the people around you, who live life in a positive state.

I challenge you to spend the next week observing positive people. Don't make personal judgements about them; simply notice how much more confident they are. Also notice how they appear to have better luck than you or those around you with a permanently negative mindset.

Many claim there is a connection between luck and self-confidence. Have you noticed that lucky people often appear to have wealth, good health, perfect relationships and achieve their goals?

Lucky people also often appear to have high levels of self-confidence. Research shows that lucky and confident people share similar characteristics and behaviours. What are you waiting for; it's time to get confident and lucky.

If you surround yourself with negative people and situations you will find it difficult to be positive and build your self-confidence. Minimise the opportunities for negative people to pull you down. If you are one of these negative people, do yourself a favour and stop.

Sometimes it's easier to blame other people for your lack of self-confidence than deal with your issues. This might work for you in the short-term but it will never help you to gain self-confidence.

Self-confidence and luck form a powerful partnership. One feeds the other. What's more, they often give you the skills to positively impact those around you.

So where does intuition sit in this heady mix?

"The intuitive mind is a sacred gift and the rational mind is a faithful servant. We have created a society that honours the servant and has forgotten the gift" - Albert Einstein

Intuition is sometimes referred to as your higher consciousness, innate intelligence, inner voice, gut feeling, hunch, or sixth sense. We all have our own way of describing it. Intuition is often described as the ability to sense or know immediately without reasoning. Call it what you like, it's the same thing.

Intuition is the feeling you get when you first hear about something. It can also be your first impression when you meet someone new. All of these are examples of your intuition. Therefore, you know much more than you realise.

By using perception and your other five senses you can tune into your intuition. Research suggests that those who pay attention can find intuition a useful tool in their lives. Obviously there is considerably more I could write about intuition, but I hope this has piqued your interest.

This exercise is designed to help you connect with your intuition. It's that little voice that you know you should listen to, but so often ignore. For a few minutes at least, please listen to your intuition.

Exercise: Connecting With Your Intuition

This exercise is an opportunity to tune into your quiet inner voice. If you learn to harness your intuition you can use it to help develop your self-confidence. You'll be pleased you did.

Simply trying this exercise once won't make you more naturally aware. However, if you do this exercise regularly you will become more aware. Once you're aware of your intuition you can start working with it.

You don't need any special equipment or resources for this mindfulness exercise. You may decide that mindfulness isn't for you, but at least give it a try before making up your mind.

1. Sit comfortably in a chair with your eyes open. If you prefer you could lie on a bed or sofa. The important thing is to feel comfortable and be able to relax for a few minutes

2. Notice any mind chatter that is going on in your head. This may be racing thoughts or a running dialogue. You could even have a stream of images running through your mind

3. Now become aware of your breathing. For the next minute or so, just notice the gentle rise and fall of your breath. Notice whether your breathing is deep or shallow

4. Now notice your body in the chair or on the bed. Feel your arms, back and legs touching the chair or bed

5. Now become aware of your blinking. Is it rapid or infrequent? Normally this would happen without you being conscious of it

6. Spend a minute (or longer if you prefer) just noticing all the sensations you're experiencing right now

7. Now reflect on how it feels to suddenly be aware of these sensations. These are automatic reflexes that you've previously been unaware of. They're innate and just happen without any conscious thought on your part

8. When you start to become naturally aware of these sensations you will also start to hear your inner voice. For some this will be a 'gut' feeling rather than a voice. It may take days, weeks or even months before you're able to hear or sense your intuition

9. Before resuming your previous activity, reflect on how you found this exercise. Was it easy or hard to do? Did you enjoy it? Will you try mindfulness again or wasn't it for you?

Your intuition (inner voice) often gets drowned out by the mind chatter. The more 'mindful' you become the quieter and calmer your mind will become. Once you've reprogrammed your brain it will assume that each time you do this exercise is quiet time.

The more you do this exercise the more in-tune you will become with your inner voice. As you become calmer and more relaxed you will find it much easier to hear your intuition talking to you. The next step will be learning to trust your intuition.

Note: you can set aside just a few minutes for this exercise. You don't need to devote hours and hours to it. Just a few minutes every day will make a difference over time.

Obviously this exercise won't work for every decision you make. However, sometimes giving your intuition a free reign will help you to reach a decision that your logical brain wouldn't have considered.

The next time you find yourself in a challenging situation try to ignore the mind chatter. Give your intuition the chance to speak and see what it's telling you.

Your self-confidence is within your control. If you take nothing else from this book, please take this key message. Other people are not responsible for your luck or self-confidence, you are. Other people may wish you well or not, or be completely indifferent to you. They may be nice or horrible to you. At the end of the day you are the only person who can control your thoughts.

An excellent way to develop your self-confidence is to allow your positive attitude to come forth. When you think positively, it will provide the impetus to overcome difficult periods when success seems like a distant dream.

"Trust yourself. You know more than you think you do" - Dr Benjamin Spock

5. Communication And Self-confidence

"Only you can make you feel less equal. Others may suggest it, but it's your choice to accept it. Find the self-confidence to say no to put-downs"
- Elizabeth J Tucker

Communication can be complex. It's both a verbal and non-verbal activity. The words you speak only play a small part in the message you convey. Communication is a combination of body language, tone of voice and actual words spoken.

So often the message you send isn't what the other person receives. Repeated miscommunication can lead to angst and may eventually erode your self-confidence. This alone is a good reason to improve your communication skills.

Effective communication is a skill that will assist in every aspect of your life. As your communication skills develop so will your self-confidence. Effective communication is a really useful skill to have in your self-confidence toolkit. I don't believe we can ever be too skilled in the art of effective communication.

First impressions are the most important impression as they're permanent. You can't recreate a first impression at a later date. On first meeting we all make judgements about physical appearance and body language. However, it doesn't stop there. We also notice the other person's energy. We decide whether they are open or closed and whether we like them or not. All this decision making in a matter of seconds!

Creating a confident first impression is important. The more confident you feel the better impression you will create. Others are also more likely to want to engage with you. Other people react or respond to the first impression you create. Aim to always create a first impression that says "this is a self-confident person".

Stop for a moment. Consider how little notice you take of somebody you regard as insignificant, compared to someone you see as powerful or charismatic. Now consider how effective you are at communicating with someone who appears unimpressed by you. This is so much harder than talking to someone who's interested in what you have to say.

If you feel confident you will create a better impression every time than if you obviously lack self-confidence. True and lasting self-confidence comes from deep within you. It's both sexy and engaging (regardless of your physical beauty).

Do you need plastic surgery, Botox or any other cosmetic procedure to feel beautiful? Are you a victim of fashion? Are you a people pleaser? If you answered yes to any of these questions your self-confidence needs tackling. These are not the ingredients for sustainable self-confidence.

Trying to change yourself to fit in, or constantly being a people pleaser is an unhealthy behaviour. In the longer-term this is likely to harm your self-confidence as you will constantly be trying to be good enough. Stop! Know that you are already good enough as you are. Create a public image of self-confidence even if it isn't true initially.

Obviously verbal communication has a big part to play in shaping the person you are. The words and phrases you use every day become your framework for how you perceive the world. It also dictates how the world perceives you. The messages you keep telling yourself have the power to build or crush your self-confidence. Scary isn't it.

In 'A Matter of Self-confidence - Part I' I discussed the common traits shared by people who lack self-confidence. Confident people share common traits too; especially when it comes to verbal communication.

When communicating are your messages usually positive or negative? If you normally choose negative or problem focused messages your brain will become programmed to notice negativity. If your language is normally positive and upbeat your brain will naturally detect positive messages and energy.

Would you say that you're better at describing your positive or negative traits? Are you ready to discover the answer? If so, try this quick exercise.

Your will need a piece of paper and a pen for this exercise. Don't spend any more than a few minutes on this exercise as your natural thinking will become obvious very quickly.

Exercise: My Positive and Negative Traits

We all have a combination of positive and negative thoughts, but we're also naturally more inclined towards positive or negative thinking. Here's your chance to find out.

1. On your sheet of paper create two columns. The headings are - 'My Positive Traits Are...' and 'My Negative Traits Are...'

2. For the next 3-5 minutes (no longer) ask yourself "what are my positive traits?" As quickly as you can, write your thoughts down. Don't spend time thinking about this or analysing your answers. Just write whatever comes into your head

3. Stop after 5 minutes. Don't look at your answers or even think about them. Move straight onto the next question

4. For the next 3-5 minutes (no longer) ask yourself "what are my negative traits?" As quickly as you can, write your thoughts down. Don't spend time thinking about this or analysing your answers. Just write whatever comes into your head

5. At the end of 5 minutes stop. Don't look at your answers or even think about them yet

6. Which list is longer? Has this surprised you?

7. Now consider your answers to both questions. Are your observations a true reflection of you, or are they just your perception at this moment?

8. If your tendency was to negative thinking it's time to work on this. Pay more attention to the language you use. Perhaps a reward and penalty system will help you to break this negative cycle of thinking. Perhaps this will be one of the actions for your action plan in chapter 9

Over the next few weeks start to observe how confident people communicate. Notice how this is different to negative people. Also notice how others respond to positive people. Here are some common communication traits of confident people:

- Confident people focus on what they want rather than what they don't want
- They talk about and focus on successes more than failures
- Their voice sounds relaxed and upbeat, not tense, monotone or downbeat

- The volume will generally be appropriate to the situation. Their voice may naturally rise and fall to enable them to make their point clearly. A high and squeaky pitch or practically whispering are not signs of self-confidence
- Confident people are generally better at pacing themselves. They don't talk so fast no-one can keep up. They don't talk so slowly you want to finish their sentences for them either
- Confident people tend to take regular pauses. This gives their audience chance to register their words and acknowledge them. Often this provides an opportunity for their words to create an impact. Watch professional or motivational speakers in action and observe how they speak
- Confident people generally demonstrate a passion for the subject they're talking about

Be clear and assertive, not passive or aggressive, in your communication. Vague, unclear messages give others an opportunity to dismiss what you're saying. Why would you want to do this? Feeling ignored or dismissed will make you feel unimportant. This often contributes to lack of self-confidence.

How often do you send out vague or ineffectual messages? Are you aware of doing it? Try the following exercise and see what you discover about your ability to send clear, positive, messages.

Exercise: My Ineffectual Messages

None of us gets it right all the time. For some people sending ineffectual messages becomes a self-confidence damaging habit. Here's a chance for you to find out how you're doing. You will need a piece of paper and a pen for this exercise.

1. Spend two minutes thinking of an occasion or occasions when your message was vague, unclear or ineffectual. Your example should be a time when you said something but the other person interpreted it differently to your intention

2. Now spend two minutes thinking about when you were at your most effective as a communicator. Think of an example where you got your message over clearly. It doesn't matter whether this was a negative or positive message. The important thing is your message was clearly understood

---

3. Think about how differently other people react to you in both of these situations. Being a good communicator doesn't mean the other person will always like what you're saying. Being a good communicator is about being understood

4. Are your poor communication skills due to lack of self-confidence? If so, think of ways to improve your communication skills. This may involve increasing your knowledge of the subject. Knowledge is a wonderful way to improve self-confidence

5. Now decide what you're going to do to improve your communication skills. Thinking about it's one thing but taking action requires effort and commitment

6. Make a commitment to this goal. On a piece of paper, write just one action you're willing to take to improve your communication skills. Now give this action a realistic target date. Put this piece of paper somewhere you will see it regularly

7. Decide what your reward will be for achieving this goal. Rewarding success is hugely important when developing self-confidence

8. Set to work and enjoy your reward when you successfully complete your action

There are many benefits to using positive language to communicate with others. Probably the most common benefits are:

- Positive language can increase your self-confidence
- Positive language increases your energy level
- You can positively influence those around you through your choice of words
- Other people will pay more attention to what you say, and develop a greater respect for you
- Often confident communication opens the door to new opportunities

There are probably many more benefits that I haven't included. The ones I've listed are designed to encourage you to improve your communication skills.

So how can you start to use more positive language in your verbal communication? One very simple thing you can do is say "remember" instead of "don't forget". Both mean the same thing but one appears more positive than the other.

Notice how many negative words or statements you commonly use. Then challenge yourself to see how many can be converted to positives.

As I've already said, there is more to communication than verbal messages. Communication is a combination of verbal and non-verbal messages. In order to be an effective and confident communicator you need to develop both sets of skills. On the plus side, effective communication is a great self-confidence builder.

If you can't express your needs assertively, or stand up for yourself, you're likely to become resentful. A lack of assertiveness also typically creates insecurity, doubt, pessimism, and lack of self-confidence.

When you learn to be assertive people will realise that you know your own mind. They will then give you more respect and be less inclined to pressurise you to do what they want.

As you earn more respect, especially from those whose opinion matters, you will feel better about yourself. The better self-image you develop the more confident you will feel. The more confident you feel the easier it will be to act assertively. This becomes a continuous cycle.

Asking for a pay-rise is one of the hardest things to do if you lack self-confidence. I'm often asked by clients how to tackle this thorny subject. My initial response is always the same... It's always a good starting point to believe you're entitled to a pay-rise. If you genuinely believe you've earnt it you will present yourself more positively.

If you believe you've earnt this pay rise it also makes the task of asking easier. If you lack self-confidence your self-limiting beliefs may prevent you accepting that you deserve a pay-rise. First you need to tackle any self-limiting beliefs you have.

People who lack self-confidence tend to avoid the subject completely or rush in. Neither is a satisfactory way to deal with this situation.

Don't just rush in with "I'd like a pay-rise...." This is an aggressive approach and may not achieve your desired outcome. Very few people respond positively to aggressive behaviour.

Instead, demonstrate your assertiveness skills. Arrange a mutually acceptable time and place for this conversation. This immediately suggests you're both busy people but this conversation is important.

Before you start, take a deep breath and tell yourself you can do this. Start the meeting start by saying "thanks for taking the time to see me". This softer and more assertive approach will ease you into the conversation. Now stay focused.

Next say something like "as you know, I've taken on some additional responsibilities in the past months/year". Explain the extra work you've taken on, and how well you're performing in the role. Evidence can be helpful at this point.

You can then go on to say something like "I've done some research and the current market value for this role is £... Therefore, I would like to ask for a pay-rise". This approach demonstrates assertiveness and suggests self-confidence. Of course I can't guarantee success, but I can tell you that you're more likely to be taken seriously.

It's important to understand that whether you're passive, aggressive or assertive there is no guarantee of a pay rise. What you're aiming to do is increase your chances of getting a pay rise. Demonstrating self-confidence and assertiveness will increase the odds in your favour.

You can ask for the pay-rise as part of your annual appraisal or at a separate meeting afterwards. Never ask before your performance appraisal in case you have a bad one. If you've had a good appraisal this will give you additional evidence to support your request. Good luck if this is one of your goals.

Body language is the other big give away when it comes to lack of self-confidence. People who lack self-confidence always take the defensive position. This may include (arms folded tightly accompanied by crossed legs).

Confident people rarely take this position unless they are offended or feeling cold. Don't automatically assume folded arms means a lack of self-confidence though. You need to look at the overall body language, tone of voice and words spoken.

Do you have trouble asking for what you want? Have you ever been offered a big opportunity but didn't know if you had the self-confidence to make it happen? Do you struggle to get people to do what you want? These are all fairly obvious signs of a lack of self-confidence.

You may be thinking that influencing has nothing to do with self-confidence, but you would be wrong. Don't be fooled into believing you have to be in a position of power to exercise influencing skills. This isn't the case at all. Anyone can develop and use influencing skills.

The receptionist you meet when you walk into any organisation will influence your initial impression of the entire organisation. Equally, if you ignore the receptionist when you go for an interview he/she will share their opinion with your future employer. Tread carefully.

A junior member of staff probably has better IT skills than some of his/her older executive colleagues. No matter how old you are or what your role is you can influence others. It just takes self-confidence and the right attitude.

Just because someone is in a senior position doesn't mean they can motivate others. Their power may only come from their job title. Influence is much more subtle than using your job title to get your own way. True influencing skills come from genuine self-confidence.

Persuasion and influence feels more comfortable for everyone involved than being told to do something. It's an assertive behaviour, which in itself is helpful. The person being persuaded feels they're a part of the decision-making process. As the influencer, you will feel more confident. Win/win outcomes always achieve the best results.

It's important to remember that others aren't motivated by the same things as you. Therefore, they probably won't be influenced by the same things as you. Successful influencing is the result of convincing others to your way of thinking. First, understand what motivates the other party.

Over the next week observe other people using their influencing skills. This can be very young children influencing their parents and siblings. It can be colleagues, family or friends. Just observe how other people get what they want. Are there any hints and tips that you can adopt? We're never too old to learn new skills.

If you lack self-confidence you may find it uncomfortable asking others to do something for you. This is particularly common in the workplace, but can apply to any aspect of your life. Do you find it easier to do things yourself, rather than find the courage to ask someone else to perform the task?

If this is you, here are some pointers to get you started:

- Before you say or do anything decide what you want. You need to be clear and explicit; otherwise you're likely to end up with something you didn't really want
- When do you need it by? If you don't make this clear, the chances are you won't get it at the right time
- Don't say anything until you're clear about what you want. You might find it helpful to rehearse what you want to say. Do this in your head so you'll feel a little more confident when you speak to the other person
- You may need to give yourself a good talking to before you speak to the other person. Remind yourself "I have the right to ask for this"
- Make sure you have the other person's attention before you start speaking. Check their body language and readiness to listen before you start. Also check you don't appear tense. Try to appear confident and relaxed. The other person will probably subconsciously mirror your body language. Mirroring is a great tool for persuading others to your way of thinking
- Assertively ask for what you want. If you sound confident you will encounter less resistance. Don't apologise or put yourself down. Be clear and check the other person understands what is required
- Speak and act as though you expect the other party to comply with your request. That's a demonstration of self-confidence

Listening has a vital role to play in effective communication. Unfortunately, listening is a skill that most of us need to work on.

If you're wondering how good your listening skills are here's a chance to assess them:

Exercise: My Listening Skills

Listening is probably the most important part of effective communication. It's a skill that most people haven't mastered sufficiently well yet. Just because you don't say a lot doesn't automatically make you a good listener.

1. Read each statement and then choose the answer that relates to you. The choices are - 'Often, Sometimes, Never'. Be honest with yourself

a. When dealing with conflict or controversial matters I always rehearse what I want to say
b. I rehearse what I'm going to say in most situations
c. I get irritated when people don't get to the point quickly
d. I think and respond to others quickly. Therefore, I tend to interrupt
e. When someone else is talking to me I often assume I know what they're going to say so don't fully listen
f. I judge others by their appearance and accent as much as what they say and do
g. I tend to pre-judge people and situations before I hear to what they have to say

2. Which response did you select most often? Were your answers mostly 'Often, Sometimes or Never'? Read the analysis below and see how this relates to you

Often: Listening really isn't your strong point is it. Are you too busy rushing through life to actually slow down and enjoy the experience? You probably miss out on some excellent communication opportunities as you don't give others a chance. Practice learning to listen. This may be hard initially but stick with it. You could be pleasantly surprised

Sometimes: your listening skills are mixed. You know what you should be doing, but probably forget sometimes. You obviously have some listening skills, so work on improving them. Identify where your weaknesses are and decide what action you're going to take

Never: You clearly feel comfortable with listening, which is a useful skill. Well done. Take care not to go to the extreme whereby you listen but rarely contribute to discussions. This would eventually erode your self-confidence. Remember, what you have to say is just as important as everyone else's opinion

3. Decide what action you're going to take. It's fine to recognise your skills, or not, but only action will improve them

4. You need to be able to recognise if your communication skills have improved. Therefore, I recommend a 3-month review. Simply repeat this exercise in 3 months' time and see what's changed

The truth about listening is it's no more difficult than not listening. It's just a different way to behave. Of course you can't apply 'real' or 'active' listening every minute of the day. If you did you wouldn't get anything done. Just make time for some 'real' or 'active' listening when there's an opportunity to do so.

Saying no is another issue for people who lack self-confidence. Do you have the self-confidence to say no when you mean no? Or, do you often find yourself saying yes because you didn't have the courage to say no? Take heart, you're not alone. We've probably all done this at some point.

The problem with not saying no is it can lead to resentment. You probably end up beating yourself up for being weak. Some people are expert manipulators and know how to make it virtually impossible to say no.

The charity collector for sick children is the classic one that's hard to say no to. They recognise this and use it to their advantage. I'm not suggesting it's not a worthy cause; I'm suggesting they use emotional blackmail to get what they want. This is a common practice.

Notice the people you interact with regularly. How many of them use emotional pressure to get you to say yes? What are you going to do about this in future?

Of course manipulation comes in many forms. It's important to be in control rather than be controlled by the manipulator. Consider each request on its own merit. If you can and want to say yes then do so. If you want to say no then develop some strategies to give you the courage to say no.

Most people find it harder to say no to friends than strangers. Generally, the better you know someone the harder it is to say no. Consider the people closest to you. Are you allowing any of them to manipulate you?

Exercise: Saying No

Sometimes it will be easier to say no than others. This exercise is about identifying when you find it easy or difficult to say no. You will need a piece of paper and a pen for this exercise.

1. Write a list of the people, situations or circumstances where saying no is easy. For example, someone you don't like, or someone selling a product or service you don't want.

2. Now write a list of the people, situations and circumstances where you find it hard or impossible to say no. These will often be the people closest to you

3. What makes it easy or difficult for you to say no?

4. Do you feel guilty when you say no to someone? Does this apply to everyone or just specific people?

5. Do you feel the need to justify your decision to say no?

6. On the whole confident people don't feel the need to justify saying no. They also tend to be more assertive when saying no. This generates fewer opportunities to be manipulated. How are you going to develop your resilience to those people who try to manipulate you into saying yes?

7. The next time someone tries to persuade you to say yes when you mean no, put your plan into action. This action plan is whatever you decided in step 6

8. Spend a few minutes reflecting on what this exercise has taught you about yourself. Were you surprised by any of your answers? If so, what surprised you?

If you want to learn to be more comfortable saying no, practice saying no in front of a mirror.

- Look into the mirror (rather like making eye contact with someone)
- Lift your chin
- Say no loudly and clearly (but don't shout). Make your voice sound strong and positive
- Now practice saying no in different tones of voice until you find one you're comfortable with. You may even like to try a submissive version and see how you appear

It's fine to say yes if you have the time or it's something you want to do. Saying yes but meaning no isn't going to help build your self-confidence.

Here are some points to consider about saying no:

- Constantly saying yes when you mean no will erode your self-confidence
- You have the right to say no without feeling guilty
- Other people have the right to say no too. Most people probably don't feel guilty saying no to you
- Saying no may take you out of your comfort zone. However, being honest from the outset is better in the long run

- Overcommitting yourself and then letting people down will damage your relationship with them. It may also damage your reputation and subsequently your self-confidence
- Taking on too much means the quality of what you deliver is lower. This won't impress the people who matter and will erode your self-confidence
- If you say yes to extra tasks at work you might add stress to the problem. Only say yes if you have the time to do what's required
- People may not like you saying no to them, but most will respect your honesty
- Being liked for being a soft-touch won't help you develop lasting self-confidence or gain respect
- Often saying no doesn't matter to the other person as much as you think it will
- Never say yes until you have all the information to make an informed decision
- Don't back down if you've already said no. Changing your mind will encourage others to manipulate you
- If you want to build lasting self-confidence always be true to yourself. Saying yes but meaning no sends a subliminal message to yourself that you're not as important as others

If you don't learn to say no people will always take advantage of your generosity. That's human nature. You're also likely to feel resentful, and this will almost certainly erode your self-confidence over time.

Please don't confuse saying no with being selfish, uncooperative or mean. Saying no is just about being true to yourself.

Honesty will help build your self-confidence. Honesty, kindness, helpfulness and generosity are all traits that confident people possess.

There really is no substitute for effective verbal and non-verbal communication. It's good for your self-confidence and it's better for those you're communicating with too. If you want to be a confident and effective communicator consider the following points:

- Before you start communicating, know what you want to achieve and why
- Get your objective anchored in your mind before your start negotiating. Otherwise you may be derailed

- Choose the right time and place for both parties. Often communication goes wrong because we plough in without thinking about whether now is the best time
- Make sure you have the other person's attention before you start speaking
- Have equal respect for yourself and the other person. Never assume that you're less important
- Actively listen to the other person. You may not agree with what he/she says but it's important to try to understand their point of view
- Be aware of the non-verbal communication between you. This is your non-verbal signals and the other person's
- Be clear and concise as no one likes a waffler. Waffling is often an indicator of lack of self-confidence. If you waffle the other person will get irritated and switch off, which may affect your self-confidence and the end result
- Try to create rapport with the other person, or find some common ground. If you can find some common ground it will be easier to reach agreement

"You probably wouldn't worry about what people think of you if you could know how seldom they do" - Olin Miller

Like most people I used to have a fear of public speaking. According to Peter Roper (... and death came third! co-author), public speaking is worse than death for many of us. Here's my story of overcoming my fear of public speaking. I'm not suggesting this will work for everyone.

Case Study: Overcoming the fear of public speaking

For many years I had been overlooked for promotion at work. The company felt I didn't promote myself enough. I felt resentful as I knew I could do the jobs I was applying for. The knock-on effect was every knock-back eroded my self-confidence a little more. This ever-decreasing spiral continued for several years. Eventually the pain became too much to bear and I decided to do something about it.

I concluded the only solution was to force myself out of my comfort zone. I realised that I rarely spoke up in meetings and wasn't comfortable with large groups. I knew I had to do something to stop this escalating.

I decided to join Breast Cancer Campaign as a Regional Volunteer. This would mean being in social situations where I didn't know anyone. It also meant I would have to give short presentations to small fundraising groups.

Fundraisers would often do events to raise money for Breast Cancer Campaign. My role was to meet the fundraisers, collect the cheque and say a few words of thanks. Even though these groups were very small, it was still a scary experience to stand up and do this initially. Like many people, public speaking terrified me. However, little by little my self-confidence grew and I got my nerves under control.

One day I was asked to attend a Bristol University Rag Week event. Unfortunately, the Breast Cancer Campaign Coordinator hadn't briefed me properly. If she had I wouldn't have gone to the event.

Imagine my surprise when I arrived to discover an audience of 200 people. Not only was I there to collect a cheque, they expected a short presentation on the work of Breast Cancer Campaign. Furthermore, mine was to be the first presentation of the night.

I had a really bad case of stage fright! At that moment all I wanted was a hole to appear in the floor. I was desperately praying for a fatal heart attack, but of course it didn't happen.

I was faced with run away and risk the donation being given to another charity. Or, fake self-confidence and stand up in front of the audience. I didn't know which was worse - telling the charity what I'd done or giving the presentation.

I got up on that stage and delivered an off-the-cuff presentation on the work of the charity. At the end of my presentation I got a standing ovation. Yes, little old me got a standing ovation. To this day, I have absolutely no idea what I said in that presentation.

Afterwards a representative from the NSPCC came up to me. He said "you're obviously a professional as that was a very polished presentation. Do you do this sort of thing often?" I said, "Yes, I do, and thank you very much it's nice to be appreciated". I knew this wasn't true, but he didn't.

Following that event in Bristol one of my friends nicknamed me 'the queen of bull..... Although not a flattering remark, it's a label that seems to have stuck.

Of course my fear of public speaking didn't just melt away, but I survived the experience. What's more, I felt incredibly proud of myself and that did wonders for my self-confidence. Other people can't make you feel good; it's something you have to do for yourself as it's an internal emotion.

Of course, like everyone else I still have the occasional self-confidence blip. The important thing is I now recognise that you don't die from lack of self-confidence. When I face a self-confidence roadblock now, I deal with it head on instead of running away.

(Liz - Overcoming the fear of public speaking author)

If you have a story about overcoming your fear of public speaking, I'd love to hear from you. Please get in touch with me at shepherdcreativelearning@gmail.com.

You can create stronger relationships by learning and practicing better ways of relating to others. It might seem silly at first to think you need to learn how to do this. Isn't it something that just happens? No. Effective communication is like any other skill, we learn and perfect it over time.

The way we communicate with others is important. This is how we let people know who we are, what we believe in, what our values are, and how we feel. The more effective your communication skills the greater your self-confidence is likely to be.

"The world only sees what you show it. If you act confidently people will assume you're confident" - Elizabeth J Tucker

6. Confident Decision Making

"In a moment of decision, the best thing you can do is the right thing to do. The worst thing you can do is nothing" - Theodore Roosevelt

Are you a great procrastinator? Do you put off making decisions for fear of making the wrong decision? If so, don't beat yourself up as you're not alone.

Often we already know what to do, but we spend hours creating good and bad scenarios in our head. It's a bit like trying to use a crystal ball to predict the outcome before making a decision. As Theodore Roosevelt put it - the worst thing you can do is nothing. Procrastination is a common trait of people who lack self-confidence.

Don't exhaust yourself trying to make the right decision. Just know that whatever decision you make it will be the right one at that time. This doesn't mean it will prove to be the right decision in future when you have more knowledge or information on the subject.

Learn to accept that not every decision you make will produce a positive outcome. Life isn't meant to be a list of perfect decisions. If it was you would learn very little from your experience here on earth. Develop the self-confidence to accept whatever happens.

There are two elements to confident decision making. These are deciding what to do and when to take action. Procrastination kills creativity and self-confidence. It also often results in nothing getting done.

I'm not suggesting you should make every significant decision on the spur of the moment, but it is important to create balance. Some decisions can be made almost instantly or without a great deal of thought. Some need considerable thought. On other occasions it's a matter of assessing the options available and then making a decision.

Everyone can make brilliant decisions, and we do so in our own way. My message to you is - stop doubting yourself! Self-doubt harms self-confidence. The ability to make decisions makes you a potentially good decision maker.

Exercise: A Good Decision Maker

We all can make good and bad decisions. Whether we're aware of it or not, we all have preconceived ideas about what makes a good and bad decision maker. This exercise is an opportunity to reflect on what you think makes a good decision maker.

1. In your opinion, what makes a good decision maker? Write a list of everything that pops into your head. This is about your perception so don't worry about whether you're right or wrong

2. What type of decision maker are you? Are you a swift or hasty decision maker? Or, do you struggle to make decisions? On the other hand, do you weigh up the pros and cons and then make an informed decision? Of course you will be each type of decision maker at separate times. However, one style is likely to be more dominant

3. Why do you find it easy or difficult to make decisions? You might like to spend a few minutes pondering this question. By understanding how you make decisions you will know whether good decision making is innate in you

4. If you struggle with decision making start with something simple. Next time you're in a restaurant or café read the menu and then challenge yourself to decide in less than 1 minute. This is a low-risk decision so it shouldn't be painful

5. By practicing with low-risk decisions you will build self-confidence. This will then equip you to make bigger decisions. When you're comfortable with low-risk decision making challenge yourself to make bigger decisions

6. What is your definition of a bad decision?

Note: In case you're struggling with question 1 - here are some typical answers my clients give me when I ask this question:

- Never being wrong
- The confidence to make assumptions when you don't have all the information needed
- Pacing the decision-making process according to how big the decision is and when it needs to be made
- The right outcome
- Ability to decide quickly when needed

If decision making seems scary to you, here are some other low-risk decisions you can start with:

- When you're shopping, find two items of clothing that you like. Choose to buy one of them only. Which one are you going to opt for?
- Write a list of holiday destinations on a sheet of paper, and then choose one
- Create a 'To Do' list and decide what order to complete the tasks
- Next time you go into a bar select a drink that you don't normally choose

These are deliberately trivial examples. Their purpose is to encourage you to feel comfortable making decisions.

Here's a little challenge for you to complete in the next week. In the next seven days make three quick decisions (nothing major). Ideally these should be things that you would normally procrastinate over. At the end of the week review your decisions. How do you feel now?

There are times when it can be useful to get a helping hand to make a confident decision. It's important not to rely on others for every decision as this will eventually erode your self-confidence. Trust yourself and only ask for help when you really need it.

Theodore C Sorensen (author of Decision-Making in the White House) was an advisor to John F Kennedy. He once said "and once I have all the options before me, then I comfortably and confidently make my decision". This is good advice for all of us.

Do you have your own formula for decision making? If not, why not adopt Michael Neill's (author of You Can Have What You Want) suggestion. He recommends using your head, heart and gut when exploring something important. This seems like a really sensible approach to me.

Here are my suggestions for using your head, heart and gut. You may have your own questions. If not, these might offer a little help to get you started.

The head:
- What do I already know about the situation (the facts)?
- What would a subject matter expert advise?
- Can anyone else help me make this decision? If so, who?

- If I need extra information, where can I find it?

The heart:
- If I was living completely by my values, what would my decision be?
- What is the kindest thing to do about this situation? This kindness may impact you or others
- If I was giving advice to a friend what would my heart be telling them to do?

The gut:
- What do I instinctively feel is the right decision?
- What do I really want to do? This is often different to doing the right thing
- How will I feel afterwards if I do what I want rather than what I know is right?
- If the decision was already made, what would it be?

The final question is - what's my decision?

Of course thinking about doing something and actually doing it are different things. Are you equally slow to take action once the decision is made? If so, your 'lifelong list of achievements' is going to be shorter than those who act.

According to Napoleon Hill (author of Think and Grow Rich) successful people make decisions quickly. He says they then change their decisions slowly, if at all. His message suggests that those who make decisions often go to the top, whereas, those who don't make decisions don't go anywhere.

Clearly this statement can't be applied to everybody. However, it provides food for thought.

Exercise: Making a Big Decision

Do you have a big decision to make and can't make up your mind what to do? If so, try this exercise. If you don't have a big decision to make right now create a fictitious scenario for this exercise.

Alternatively, think of a big decision you've made historically. Use this exercise to see if you would have made the same or a different decision. Generally, I would say that hindsight is not a good thing, but you're only using hindsight for the purpose of this exercise. Don't use this exercise as an excuse for self-criticism.

1. For the purpose of this exercise just focus on your big decision. This exercise is not about your life generally

2. Get a large sheet of paper - A4 is ideal for this exercise. Divide the page into four squares

3. The headings for the four squares are - Do and Gain, Do and Lose, Don't and Gain, Don't and Lose (see example below)

Do and Gain	Do and Lose
Don't and Gain	Don't and Lose

4. Start with Do and Gain. In this square write down anything you can expect to gain by acting. Your list may have multiple gains. Gains may include self-confidence or new opportunities

5. Next look at Do and Lose. In this square write a list of the things you might lose by acting. Think broadly and creatively. For example - lose a friendship, lose credibility, lose money etc

6. When you're ready move onto Don't and Gain. Is doing nothing an option? If so, what or why would you gain from doing nothing? Note: this is not generally a good choice, but sometimes it can be

7. Finally consider Don't' and Lose. Now it's time to think of the consequences of doing nothing. The example that pops into my head is ignoring the letter from Her Majesty's Revenue and Customs. If you ignore their letters you're likely to end up with a fine

I'm not suggesting that every decision needs such structured consideration. However, on occasions it can be helpful to weigh up the pros and cons before making a decision.

Of course you can't predict the future and you won't make the right decision every time. Learn to trust your ability to make good decisions. This will help develop your self-confidence. If you make an unwise decision, accept it, learn from it and move on.

Of course not every decision is good or bad. Many of the decisions you make every day are just neutral decisions. Nothing earth shattering is going to happen if you have toast for breakfast instead of a bowl of cereals. However, you still made a decision about which to have. The thing about decision making is, try not to make it a personal mountain to climb.

Why not make a good decision right now. Create a bucket list of all the things you want to do before you die. You can add to or alter your bucket list at any time; the important thing is to get started. These can be very big or small activities or experiences.

One of the items on my bucket list was a promise to have a trip on a steam train. It didn't need to be anything lavish and expensive; just a ride on a steam train. Since starting to write this book I've ticked this off my bucket list, and I thoroughly enjoyed it.

Like any other goal setting exercise, completing a task provides motivation. Success and motivation lead to increased self-confidence. What are you waiting for? If you don't already have a bucket list, now is a good time to start one. If you already have one, review it and add to it.

Exercise: My Bucket List Goal

Bucket lists are a great long-term goal setting tool. It's good to have dreams and aspirations. Some of the items on your bucket list may not get done, and that's fine. Further down the line, you may wish to change some of your bucket list goals. That's fine too. For now, simply choose one of the goals on your bucket list for this exercise.

1. Look at your bucket list and make a commitment to turn one of these aspirations into a tangible goal. Spend a few minutes just looking at your list until your intuition guides you to the right one

2. When you've decided what your goal is write the heading on a sheet of paper. You have now made your first decision regarding this goal

3. Write the details of what this goal looks like to you. Be as specific as possible

4. Define why this goal is on your bucket list. This will help strengthen your desire to do it

5. What is your target date? Commit to this target date for achieving this goal. You've now made another decision

6. Write a list of the things you need to do to achieve this goal. When are you going to start? There are two more decisions made

7. Consistently work towards achieving your goal. When you've succeeded remember to reward yourself. Rewards are very important in self-confidence building

Note: you may want to make increased self-confidence one of your bucket list goals. If so, remember to decide what your target level of self-confidence is going to be.

Moving on... What is your definition of a bad decision? You might like to spend a few minutes contemplating this question.

Disappointment in the outcome doesn't mean you made a bad decision. Too often people damage their own self-confidence by criticising themselves when something doesn't work out how they wanted.

This doesn't mean you made a bad decision. Just know that at the time you made the right decision. It's important to remember sometimes things don't go the way we wish. That's life!

Confident people focus on the process not the outcome. This is a much healthier attitude to decision making. Confident people accept that their life will be a combination of good and bad decisions. Don't obsess about either. You've got a life to live.

If you make your decision the right way and for the right reason, it's a good decision regardless of the outcome. Revisit your decision-making skills. Consider how you define good and bad decisions. Is your judgement based on the process or the outcome?

Spend a few minutes reflecting on some of the decisions you've made in the last 12 months. Categorise them as good, bad or neutral (little or no impact) decisions. How quickly did you make these decisions? Were you pleased with how you handled these decisions?

On reflection, do you believe you have good decision-making skills?

"Refuse to be pigeonholed or labelled. Your life choices are immense and the decision making intense, but feel proud to be you" - Elizabeth J Tucker

7. Dealing With Conflict, Confrontation And Bullies

"Always remember you are braver than you believe, stronger than you seem, and smarter than you think" - Christopher Robin

I can't sum it up better than Christopher Robin. Imagine a life where you never have to deal with conflict or confrontation. Wouldn't that be wonderful. Unfortunately, it's virtually impossible to avoid conflict and confrontation totally.

Conflict often brings your self-confidence, or lack of it, to the fore. The way you appear to deal with those confronting you will send a message about your power and self-confidence. The good news is there are some things you can do to help yourself in this situation. Here are some tips for your self-confidence toolkit.

Breathing - keep your breathing slow, measured and deep. You will need to practice this as the natural human reaction to confrontation is quick short breaths. This will make you more anxious and really doesn't help in conflict and confrontation situations.

By slowing your breathing down you're giving yourself a chance to think. Breathe in to a count of five. Hold your breath for a count of three to five and then breathe out to a count of five. Of course it isn't always possible to do this, but if you can it will help.

Eye contact - no matter how reluctant you feel; some eye contact is essential. Keep your eye contact steady and relaxed. Don't stare as this is likely to make both of you feel uncomfortable.

If you need to divert your gaze for a moment, look above or to the side of the other person's eyes. Avoid looking down as this immediately suggests a lack of self-confidence and may encourage the other person to be more aggressive.

It's natural to blink more when you're feeling stressed or under pressure. As we all know, conflict and confrontation can be stressful. Therefore, it's common to find yourself blinking more. Excessive blinking will tell the other person you feel under pressure. Try not to blink excessively.

Stay centred - if you're naturally uncomfortable with conflict or confrontation you may feel panicky, lightheaded or slightly dizzy in these situations. These feelings will increase as your stress level increases. Don't panic.

In moments of conflict or confrontation focus on your solar plexus (the area between the rib cage and the navel). Imagine a big yellow ball of energy sitting around your solar plexus. Imagine this ball of energy as a heavy weight. Now imagine that it's keeping you steady and grounded.

Also focus on your feet. Imagine your feet firmly rooted into the ground. If it helps, imagine how deep the roots of a big tree are. Visualise your feet pinned to the ground by good strong roots. This will help you to stay centred.

Self-talk - In a very gentle and soothing tone talk to yourself. Tell yourself "I'm OK. I'm going to get through this". "I will be fine". "I can do this". Or, choose any other personal mantra that works for you.

If you already have the skills to handle conflict and confrontation assertively, then that's great news. If you're not naturally confident in conflict or confrontation situations start by trying to 'be brave 20 seconds at a time....' I took this quote is from 'We Bought A Zoo'. It just seems so apt for this chapter.

Like every other part of your self-confidence journey, learning to cope with conflict and confrontation takes time. Treat yourself with patience and kindness as you develop assertiveness skills and new self-confidence.

Exercise: Deal With Conflict - Be Brave 20 Seconds At a Time

If we're honest, most of us don't like conflict or confrontation. However, some people seem able to take it in their stride while others shrink away from it. If the latter describes you try being brave for 20 seconds at a time.

This exercise can be done as a visualisation, but you may prefer to write your thoughts down. The choice is yours.

1. Think of a conflict or confrontation situation that you have been involved in. It doesn't matter whether this is recent or very old. Think

about your physical reaction, your emotional state and how you felt afterwards.

For example, did you have sweaty palms? Did your mind freeze, which prevented you giving the answers you would have liked to give etc? Afterwards did you think of all the things you wish you'd said?

2. On reflection, how would you have liked to handle this situation? Is there anything specific you wish you had said or done? Were you as dignified as you would have like to be? Did you give the impression of being confident or did you appear cowed by your opponent?

Note: steps 1 and 2 may have created some unhappy memories. A key element of self-confidence building is facing your demons. Please don't give up just because this exercise feels uncomfortable

3. If steps 1 and 2 have made you feel uncomfortable take a few minutes down time. When you're ready take a deep breath and carry on

4. Now tell yourself that you are going to be brave 20 seconds at a time. That's enough time to make a decision and take a giant leap of faith. If it helps, tell yourself this is just 20 seconds of insane courage. Twenty seconds out of a lifetime is no more than a raindrop

5. Revisit the scenario from step 1 again. This time see yourself handling the situation confidently. Notice how the other person reacts differently to the new, more confident, you. Remind yourself that you only have to be brave 20 seconds at a time. Each 20 seconds moves you closer to the end of the encounter

6. Tell yourself that this memory no longer has the power to intimidate you. Then let the memory go. Imagine this painful memory drifting off into the clouds

7. In future if you find yourself in a conflict/confrontation situation take a deep breath and be brave for 20 seconds. Use your 20 seconds to tell yourself you can do this and think of a suitable response to your aggressor. Imagine this as a marathon not a sprint. See yourself winning the battle

8. Throughout the encounter, remind yourself to be brave 20 seconds at a time. This will stop you making knee jerk reactions (the sprint mentality), and rushing to blindly answer your aggressor

9. When the encounter is over allow yourself a few minutes of peace and calm before moving onto your next task. A few deep breaths will help.

Use this time to give yourself a virtual pat on the back. Know that you have just taken another step towards self-confidence

When you're faced with a conflict or confrontation situation it can be more effective to say very little. When you do speak, keep your sentences short and don't get defensive. Say things like "I don't agree..." or "that's incorrect..."

Make sure your tone is firm and confident but don't sound sharp or aggressive. Also, never sound nervous or intimidated. Try to speak at your normal volume, as this will help to fool your aggressor into believing you're fine with this. He/she may be looking for clues like a change of tone of voice. Don't give him/her the satisfaction.

Avoid making personal comments and bringing up historical issues. Instead, smile at your aggressor. There is nothing more unsettling than being smiled at by the person you are insulting. It sends a message that says "you can't upset me".

All in all, less really is more in conflict situations. The less you say the more your aggressor will have to say. This will probably lead to them saying things they later regret, and may even harm their credibility. If someone wants to be aggressive or confrontational, let them but don't stoop to their level. Just keep being brave for 20 seconds at a time.

Of course conflict situations are unpleasant. Hopefully they won't be a common occurrence in your life. When you've faced the situation, do take a few minutes to be proud of how you handled yourself. This is probably one of the biggest building blocks in your wall of self-confidence.

It doesn't matter who you're dealing with, the rules are the same. Use the same approach with family, friends, colleagues, customers or even strangers. If you react to aggression with aggression you will just make matters worse. Assertiveness is far more effective than aggressive or passive behaviour in conflict situations.

The key ingredients for successfully handling conflict situations are - respect, fairness, assertiveness, active listening and a positive attitude. Each of these will help create an impression of self-confidence. You may not be feeling confident but pretend you are. Remember the old saying - 'fake it till you make it'.

Hopefully you won't have to deal with conflict or confrontation often, but it helps to have a strategy just in case. I use the following ten rules for handling conflict and confrontation situations.

Rule 1: Take a few deep breaths before you say or do anything. This gives you a few seconds of thinking time and may prevent you saying something you regret

Rule 2: Remain as calm as possible. If you lose control of yourself, you hand your power to the other person. He/she will then be in a position to control or manipulate you. If you feel out of control, do an emergency stop. Take a deep breath. Next, think and say some positive words (even if you don't want to)

Rule 3: Hear the person out. Never attempt to manage an angry person until you've given them chance to let off steam. He/she won't be ready to listen until they've vented their anger. Someone once said "a barking dog can't bite". Think about it - this is so true!

Rule 4: Listen, without interrupting, to what the other person is saying before attempting to sort out the issue. Your perception of what he/she wants is almost certain to be different to their perception. Try to put yourself in the other person's shoes. This isn't so you can agree with them, but so you can empathise with them

Rule 5: Use positive, calming body language and continue to breathe deeply. This will stop you looking as if you're up for a fight. If you get this right the other person will mirror your body language

Rule 6: Pace yourself. Don't speak too fast or too slowly, as both will aggravate the other person. Always remember you're trying to control the situation not the person

Rule 7: Always look for a win/win outcome. Once you start trying to win it becomes a fight. You will achieve a better outcome if both parties feel they've won something

Rule 8: Remember you can't control the other persons' attitude so don't bother trying. Instead, focus on controlling your own attitude, body language and verbal communication skills. When the words are spoken they can't be retracted

Rule 9: Don't take the other person's anger personally. Most times the anger is about the situation not you. Even if it is designed as a personal attack, don't allow the other person to attack your self-confidence. Stay focused on achieving a positive outcome

Rule 10: If you feel yourself becoming angry, stop the conversation. If possible take a short break. If you can't take a break try to steer the conversation in a different direction. As I've already said, losing self-control gives power to the other person

Note: if you apply rule 3, you will find some people resolve the situation for themselves. Not everyone wants you to provide the solution. Some just need to vent their anger.

Dealing with tricky situations assertively is a fantastic way to build your self-confidence. Some people can deal with difficult customers but not family, friends, colleagues or bosses. Others can deal with difficult colleagues but not customers, and so it goes on. We're all different.

Is there a particular group or situation you find it harder to deal with? If you're aware of it you can prepare for this. Is there a particular group or situation that you manage confidently? If so, consider how you do it and what skills you can use for more challenging situations.

The following exercise is an opportunity to reflect on how you manage difficult people or situations.

Exercise: Managing Difficult People or Situations

Confidently dealing with tricky situations is a skill. It's a useful skill to have, and one that will help you in all areas of your life.

Read and truthfully answer the following questions. Like all confidence building, sometimes confronting your weaknesses can be uncomfortable. Remember, dealing with your weaknesses builds self-confidence.

You will need a piece of paper and a pen for this exercise.

1. What do you do when you're successfully handling tricky situations? Think about your body language, tone of voice, vocabulary etc. Do you feel in control of the situation? Do you have a particular technique for calming these situations?

2. Do you handle these situations well because you're feeling confident? Or, have you trained yourself to hide your lack of self-confidence and handle the situation positively?

3. What do you do differently in the tricky situations you don't handle so well? Compare your answers from questions 1 and 3

4. In which situations are you most likely to lose control?

5. When you lose self-control do you make your attack personal? Do you lash out at the other person with personal comments?

6. How do you feel about your outburst afterwards? Do you feel embarrassed, ashamed, or do you justify your behaviour to yourself? Do you keep replaying it in your mind?

7. How do you feel when you've confidently and assertively dealt with a tricky situation or person? Do you keep replaying it in your mind, or do you forget about it and move on?

8. How can you transfer your skills from question 1 to deal with all tricky situations assertively? Think about how differently you behave

9. What have you learnt about yourself from this exercise? Hopefully you have positive, neutral and negative observations

10. What will you do differently in future?

Often conflict and confrontation take us by surprise. This doesn't give you time to prepare. If you know in advance that you have a difficult matter to discuss you can prepare for it. Make notes of the points you wish to raise and think about the best ways to approach the situation.

Your chances of a successful outcome are better if you can assertively take control of the situation from the outset. Always feel confident enough to stand your ground. Don't be bullied or intimidated. Always remember, you have the same rights as the other person.

It's important to get your tone of voice and body language right. If you start the conversation with aggression the other person will almost certainly respond aggressively. The chances of a positive outcome are then very slim.

Not all conflict or confrontation is a single outburst. All too often it can be an element of an ongoing bullying situation. Let's be honest, when you're on the receiving end of bullying it's an awful experience. Bullying can destroy whatever self-confidence you currently have.

If you're being bullied it probably won't help to know that bullying can be a front for lack of self-confidence. Often bullies conceal their lack of self-confidence by being a bully. As the victim you may feel extremely uncomfortable at the thought of challenging the bully. This it completely understandable, so don't beat yourself up about it.

Bullying can occur in almost any setting. For the purpose of this book I'm not addressing domestic bullying/abuse. Domestic bullying/abuse is a complex issue and would fill an entire book on its own. I have touched on workplace bullying though. You may like to know that workplace bullying is part of our self-confidence home study programme.

Sadly workplace bullying is not uncommon. Imagine that your manager or a colleague keeps putting your down at work. Over time this is bound erode your self-confidence. If this isn't dealt with it could have a debilitating effect on you.

No one should ever be bullied at work. There is never any excuse for this behaviour. What's worse, workplace bullying often goes unchallenged. There are lots of reasons for this. The most common reason is the victim doesn't report it to someone who can help.

If workplace bullying isn't reported and tackled the victim often ends up leaving his/her job. Too often this doesn't fix the problem.

Wherever the bullying takes place it takes enormous courage to stand up to a bully. Don't underestimate how brave you've been when you do this. If you're considering challenging a bully here are some pointers:

- Acknowledge your fear and the harm it's doing to your self-confidence
- Keep a record (including the date and time) every time the bullying occurs. This record will be useful if you have to make a formal complaint
- Ask yourself what you're scared of. Typically the answer is being publicly humiliated
- Try to understand why the bully is behaving in this way. Is it because he/she lacks self-confidence, doesn't like you etc
- This is not intended to excuse or justify the bullying behaviour. It's a way of helping you to find the self-confidence to tackle the issue
- It's generally very difficult to deal with this person on your own. Find a buddy or support network before you tackle the bully
- Challenge the perpetrator. In most cases the shock of being accused of bullying will stop the bully in his/her tracks. How many of us would ever be proud of being accused of bullying?
- If the bullying doesn't stop make a formal complaint. Provide evidence when you make the complaint. This makes it easier and quicker for the company to deal with the matter

In any bullying situation there are three parties. These are - the person who is being bullied, the bully, and the people who watch it happening. The observers should as ashamed as the bully as they allow it to go on.

If you are the victim, be kind to yourself and deal with the situation in stages. First, have compassion for yourself, and tell yourself this is not your fault. Find a positive mantra and keep repeating it.

Even very skilled, personable and competent people can become prey to a bully. Don't be fooled into thinking bullying only happens to very quiet people, or those who are different in some way. This is not the case. Anyone can become the victim of a bully.

Never underestimate the detrimental effects of bullying. Bullying has a hugely undermining effect on self-confidence. Always remember you're not to blame for the bullying, but you can do something about it.

If this bullying has been ongoing for some time you already know that others won't do anything about it. Unfortunately, you've already seen them turn a blind eye. Going down the route of least resistance (accepting the situation) will not lead to a happy outcome. The bullying is likely to get worse.

If the bullying is taking place at work, you may decide to leave your job. This will remove you from the clutches of this bully, but it doesn't deal with the emotional damage caused. Even if you leave your job, the experience will have done significant harm to your self-confidence.

If you don't deal with your bullying situation there is a good chance that it will happen again somewhere else. Your self-confidence will be low, which seems to send a signal to other bullies. Don't give bullies the upper hand as you have no control over how or when the bullying will occur.

Another good reason to tackle bullying is the potential health issues it can cause. In extreme cases the health issues can be serious, including depression.

Someone close to me became an insulin dependent type 1 diabetic as a result of bullying that wasn't stopped. If only she could have seen what the future held, perhaps things would have been different. It's better to confront the situation than look back afterwards and wish you'd handled things differently.

Know that you deserve to have your self-confidence back. Every small step you take to increase your self-confidence is worth the effort. The best way to achieve a big goal is to take small steps in the right direction. Dealing with bullying is no different.

If you've ever been the victim of bullying reflect on how good you felt after you successfully dealt with the situation. I hope you feel very proud of your achievement. You have every reason to be proud of dealing with this situation and your tormentor.

You may not have previously realised that this horrible experience increased your self-confidence. If you can deal with something this unpleasant then some of your other self-confidence issues pale into insignificance.

I'm not suggesting that standing up to a bully is easy. Initially it can be just as painful as the bullying itself. It does get easier though. Each step you take will make you stronger. This new inner strength is your self-confidence growing. Know that at the end of the process you will feel very proud of yourself, and rightly so!

When you're being bullied you probably feel like no-one understands. This isn't the case. Most people don't share their bullying experiences as they feel ashamed or vulnerable. Here is a case study from a brave lady who has been kind enough to share her story for this book. I hope this story will give you hope.

Case Study: Dealing with a workplace bully

In the early 1990s I was working for a large national company. I was going through a difficult period in my personal life and so wasn't the best of company at this time.

I was very quiet and withdrawn, but I joined in general conversations at work. I just didn't participate in any conversations of a deeply personal nature. I didn't want to share my private life with my colleagues. I'm not that sort of person.

On reflection, I realise that I may have appeared aloof or snooty. This wasn't my intention, I was just hurting badly. I have never been someone who does my dirty washing in public. I don't believe my quietness was justification for the workplace bullying I suffered.

Part of my humiliation came from my colleagues watching this daily verbal assault take place. No one on the team said a word. They would either give me pitying looks or bury their heads in their work and pretend they were unaware.

My tormentor was my team leader, and so difficult to avoid. At first I hoped it was a temporary thing and would go away. Of course it didn't. After a couple of months of regular bullying I spoke to my tormentor privately about her anti-social behaviour.

I hoped this would address the issue, but it didn't. Instead it made things worse. She started overtly ridiculing me in front of colleagues. It eventually became the worst kept secret on the team. Still no one was willing to pitch in and help. What's more, no one wanted to be seen to support me in any way. At its worst, the rest of the team tried not to be seen talking to me.

This carried on for nine miserable months. Finally something inside me snapped and I decided enough was enough. I spent an entire weekend drafting and redrafting my grievance. I don't remember how many times I redrafted that document. Late on the Sunday night I felt that I had a coherent statement. I was ready to fight back...

First thing on Monday morning I asked for a private meeting with my supervisor. I felt nauseous; I was shaking with nerves and had a blinding headache. I knew it was now or never. My supervisor immediately took me to a private meeting room.

As soon as we sat down I launched my attack. I didn't want my courage to abandon me now. After all it had taken so long to get to this point. I didn't stop until the whole statement was read.

I told my supervisor I wished to make a formal grievance about my team leader. I also said that I wished to read a prepared statement to her. As I read she looked stunned but listened to me without interrupting. When I'd finished she let me have a short cry.

She then took charge of the situation. My biggest fear was I wouldn't be believed. This didn't happen. She took my statement and asked me to take a short break before going back to my desk.

Feeling temporarily bolstered, I made it clear that if she didn't deal with the matter I was going to HR. I needn't have worried as it didn't come to that. I didn't know what was going to happen at this stage; I just had to trust her to do the right thing.

When I returned to my desk my team leader, supervisor and the department manager were missing. They were actually absent for a couple of hours. That got the team speculating on what was going on.

When they returned my team leader picked up her handbag and left the office. I didn't know at the time, but that was to be the last time I would ever see her.

My team leader was suspended, pending an investigation. Of course once I stood up to my bully everyone suddenly wanted to talk to me. They wanted all the grisly details of my complaint and happily talked about the previous nine months and their observations. For me, it was too little, too late. I never did confide in any of my colleagues.

Although this investigation was started it didn't go far. While my team leader was suspended she submitted her resignation. The company accepted it and allowed her to leave without working her notice period.

To this day, I remain hugely grateful to my supervisor. She believed me and acted on my grievance. She handled the situation very discreetly, and as such I was never asked to defend my claim.

I had a fresh start on a different team, but I was never really happy working in that office. Eventually I moved way to a different part of the country and had a fresh start.

I wish I hadn't allowed the bullying to continue for so long. My team leader made my life an absolute misery for nine months.

Although this experience was truly awful, never again have I allowed anyone to destroy my self-confidence in this way. It did build my self-confidence in a way other, more positive, experiences couldn't. If my self-confidence ever dips now I just remind myself that I have the strength to deal with anything.

I hope my bully learnt something from this experience, and has changed her behaviour. Of course, I'll never know.

(Jane - Dealing with a workplace bully author)

If you're currently being bullied or even observing it happening to someone else, you might like to try this exercise.

Exercise: Confronting The Bully

Bullying often starts very subtly. At first you may doubt your judgement. You may convince yourself that it's your imagination, or even blame yourself. You may try telling yourself that you have caused this bullying by something you said or did. It's not your fault!

Note: This exercise may be painful. However, if you are currently experiencing bullying, this may give you the courage to deal with it.

1. If your bullying is occurring in the workplace start by keeping a log. Write down the date, place, situation and words spoken. Do this every time something happens or is said to you.

Once you start to do this you will recognise a pattern of behaviour. Hopefully this evidence will give you the confidence to tackle it

2. Whatever your personal bullying situation, ask yourself the following questions.

3. Is the bullying just verbal, or does it have a physical element too? Does this bullying take place in front of other people?

4. When it happens how does it make you feel and behave?

5. How long has this been going on? Are you ready to tackle it?

6. What changes do you want to see? What is the outcome you want?

7. How would you feel if this stopped? What difference would this make to your life?

8. Do you have a confidence buddy or support network you can confide in?

Only you will know when you feel ready to tackle your tormentor. By working through these questions you will gain the self-confidence to confront the bully. A 'buddy' can be a great help as bullying can be a lonely experience. A 'buddy' will provide support when your courage needs a little help.

Remember, you don't deserve to be abused in this way. You have a right to confront this person about his/her unacceptable behaviour. When you're ready hold your head high, put your shoulders back and take a deep breath. The journey to success has just begun.

Some people prefer to speak to the bully first. They hope to nip this in the bud without involving other people. Others prefer to make a formal complaint. This could involve going to your Manager, Human Resources Department or Trade Union Representative in the case of workplace bullying. In other situations it could involve an external party or even the police.

Ideally the person or organisation you report this to would prefer you to speak to the bully first. Don't feel pressured into doing this. You need to do what feels right for you. After all, the chances are that other people are already aware that you're being bullied.

If you can't confront your bully don't feel that you're a coward. You're not. The nature of the situation makes it impossible for some people to deal with it. Just know you have 'a right not to be bullied'. You also have the right to ask for help, and get it.

Seek help as soon as possible, as the situation is unlikely to resolve itself. You may prefer to start by confiding in someone you trust. Although this person can't make the formal complaint for you, he/she will help boost your self-confidence. If you're feeling nervous about what you want to say, practice on the person you confided in.

If someone has been identified as a workplace bully then your employer has a responsibility to deal with the situation. No responsible employer will dismiss your complaint or simply ignore it. I hope this will give you the courage needed if this is your situation.

It may not help to know this but, bullying is often a symptom of lack of self-confidence. I know to the victim it looks quite the opposite. Bullies may have a reason for their unacceptable behaviour, but it still needs to be stopped.

Never turn a blind eye to bullying. Whether you're the victim, bully or an observer, stamp out bullying before someone else becomes a victim.

If you are a bully, take a long hard look at yourself. I hope you have the grace to feel ashamed. Get some help to deal with your pattern of unacceptable behaviour before it escalates into something more serious.

If you're an observer of bullying don't just ignore it. Offer the victim some help and support to stop the bullying. If necessary make someone in authority aware of the situation. Remember, you too could easily become a victim of bullying.

"Next time someone tries to make you feel bad say - you know if you felt good about yourself you wouldn't need to 'diss' me". This will take the wind out of their sails, whether they admit it to you or not - Elizabeth J Tucker

8. Make Self-confidence Your New Best Friend

"It's vital to believe in yourself. If you don't you won't have the self-confidence to keep going" - Elizabeth J Tucker

In order to achieve sustainable self-confidence you need to be committed to this goal. In short, self-confidence needs to be your new best friend. This is a lifelong commitment so be prepared for a long, but enjoyable, journey. Potentially every experience can positively contribute to your self-confidence toolkit. Yes, even the bad ones.

We all have our own personal self-confidence toolkit. Some toolkits are better equipped than others. Your self-confidence toolkit needs lots of different strategies and tools. Some you may never use, while others you will need at various times in your life.

If you stop your commitment to self-confidence, over time it will reduce or disappear. If you genuinely want to be the confident, beautiful, soul you were always destined to be, read on. Here are some rules:

- Treat yourself well (as well as, or better than, you treat others)
- Be kind to yourself - a little self-nurturing goes a long way in terms of self-confidence
- Eliminate the self-destructive critical messages that play out in your head
- Be grateful for everything in your life (the people, good health, sense of humour and experiences etc). The more grateful you feel the more good experiences you will notice and manifest
- Value yourself and recognise your skills. Don't view this as ego; it's just a matter of taking an objective view
- Reward every success (even if it's just a virtual pat on the back)
- Dig deep and know that even your negative experiences will help build your self-confidence
- Remember, if you do what you've always done you will get the same results
- Spot new opportunities and embrace all that life has to offer

Although self-confidence is a goal and requires commitment, you don't need to apply regimental discipline to it. Achieving self-confidence is a journey not a destination.

Maintaining self-confidence is a beautiful and harmonious experience. Sustainable self-confidence will give you a greater sense of wellbeing. It impacts every aspect of your life and can make your life so much better.

Being confident is about taking the initiative rather than politely waiting to be asked. Which of the following statements describes you? Be honest with yourself.

1. Do you usually wait for other people to build your self-confidence?

2. Do you believe those who don't ask don't get what they want? Do you push yourself forward and always achieve your goals?

3. Do you choose either answer 1 or 2 depending on the situation?

4. Do you take responsibility for your own self-confidence? Do you believe in yourself and your ability without an overinflated sense of self-importance?

Analysis:

1. If your answer was 1 - you're probably missing out on some of life's opportunities. Most people are too busy getting on with their own life to put you first. Choose some non-threatening situations and start to assert yourself. As your self-confidence grows push yourself a little more and see what opportunities become available to you

2. If your answer was 2 - you may be creating the impression of being prince or princess pushy. Too much 'being out there' is a demonstration of arrogance, rather than genuine self-confidence. Try to get the balance right. Self-confidence will still allow you to succeed, just less aggressively

3. If your answer was 3 - your self-confidence seems to ebb and flow. Start by identifying the areas of your life where you currently lack self-confidence. Then create an action plan to tackle your self-confidence issues. Look for opportunities to develop your self-confidence in areas where you're not as strong

4. If you answer was 4 - you obviously recognise that only you can develop your self-confidence. You appear to have genuine self-confidence. Keep looking for ways to maintain this healthy state of mind. Identify your weaker areas and work on these

Self-confidence is about asserting yourself to achieve something. It's not about getting one-upmanship over someone else. Any time you have doubts about whether you're being genuinely confident or not ask yourself 'am I being assertive, passive or aggressive'. Identify whether you're demonstrating assertiveness and self-confidence, arrogance or a lack of self-confidence.

You will need a variety of tools and strategies in your self-confidence toolkit. Before we go any further, consider these questions... "What strategies and tools do I currently have in my self-confidence toolkit? What else do I need?" I believe every self-confidence toolkit needs assertiveness, laughter and an ability to manage conflict as a bare minimum.

Assertiveness: This is essential for everybody's self-confidence toolkit. When you feel confident you're naturally assertive, express yourself more clearly, and respect other people's views. A lack of self-confidence is far more likely to result in aggressive or passive behaviour.

When you feel confident you're in the middle of the seesaw (the point of balance). However, when you lack self-confidence you probably switch between 'fight' and 'flight'. Fight is the aggressive behaviour and flight is the passive behaviour. Neither are helpful behaviours and they won't increase your self-confidence and often don't achieve the desired result.

It's important to deal with negative situations as soon as possible. This decision is a demonstration of assertiveness. Storing up angst or negative thoughts allows negative experiences to build up in your 'cell memory'. This will eventually eat into your self-confidence.

Imagine your mind as a sponge. Your mind keeps absorbing all this negative stuff until one day the sponge becomes saturated and starts leaking. This often results in an outburst where you say things you don't mean or never intended to say.

Does this sound familiar? You may have been the recipient or the perpetrator of such an outburst. Whichever role you played, the chances are it impacted you in some way. Self-confidence can be very fragile. Treat it with care and respect.

Can you remember a time when you had an outburst? Do you remember how your body felt at the time (e.g. tense)? Do you remember your tone of voice and choice of words? Were you deliberately trying to inflict emotional pain on the other person? Do you remember how the other person responded to your outburst?

Can you remember a time when you were on the receiving end of an emotional outburst? Do you remember the other person's body language and tone of voice during the outburst? How did this verbal attack make you feel? Has it left a lasting effect on you?

The chances are the perpetrator (you or another person) was just lashing out. Perhaps the perpetrator was blaming the other party for something that had happened. Alternatively, you/he/she may have been trying to justify a sense of righteousness. Whatever the reason, it was probably an unpleasant experience for both of you.

Are you left with lingering memories following any kind of unpleasant encounter? If you're self-confidence is low or fragile any kind of conflict will make you feel worse. The more confident you feel the more resilient you will be to anything unpleasant; not just conflict situations. Self-confidence is a great friend to have; it allows you to learn and move on quickly.

Here's Jasmine's case study. She kindly agreed to have her story published to demonstrate that assertiveness would have been a better way to behave.

Case Study: Passive behaviour that led to an outburst

I chose to be a stay-at-home mum when our children were small. When the children grew up I didn't return to work. If I'm honest this was largely due to lack of self-confidence. However, I disguised it as "I couldn't stand working for anyone as I'm used to doing what I like, when I like".

For years I have cooked, cleaned, decorated, done the garden and generally taken care of my family. I feel as though I'm constantly putting everyone else first. When I want to do something and ask for my family's help they just say "oh, it's another of mum's hobbies". I feel my husband and children don't take me seriously.

On reflection I realise that I frequently experience resentment, disappointment and frustration. Mostly I say nothing as I want my family to show some interest in me without being prompted. Of course they don't. To everyone I'm David's wife and Sasha and Daniel's mum. No one sees me as Jasmine - the individual.

For far too long I've chosen not to assert myself. However, recently I felt enough was enough. It was something quite trivial that created my outburst... One of my children didn't put their cup in the dishwasher and I totally overreacted. The family pointed out that I was overreacting. I knew this was true, but I was releasing a build-up of years and years of resentment.

I now realise that I've allowed myself to become passive over many years. It's hard to change this situation now, but I'm working on it. I've realised that I need to make my family aware of how I feel if things are to change. I need to learn assertiveness skills, which sounds daft at my age.

At first it was uncomfortable explaining that I felt I was giving much more than I get in return. I needed to help my husband and children understand what I want from them. Otherwise things won't ever get better. It's early days but things are slowly improving.

This was a difficult conversation for all of us initially. I'm glad I eventually plucked up the courage though, even if I did it the wrong way. I'm learning to be assertive instead of passive. It's helped us, as a family, bypass the barriers of resentment. Little by little things are getting better.

The best bit is my self-confidence is growing and my husband likes the new me. Actually, I'm probably not a 'new me', I'm probably just going back to the confident girl he married. Only now do I realise how much we take self-confidence for granted. I won't lose it again.

Jasmine (Passive behaviour that led to an outburst author)

How often do you take the opportunity to reflect on your stored up angst? Most of us try to bury these feelings as it's easier than dealing with the issues. Sooner or later these feelings are going to well up and need to be addressed.

As part of your self-confidence plan try to remove angst as soon as it appears. Saved up angst will certainly impact your self-confidence and may even harm your health. Are you currently storing up angst? Here's a chance to find out.

Exercise: Saved Up Angst

This exercise is an opportunity to reflect on your saved up angst. Once you're aware of this you can decide what action, if any, you want to take.

1. Write down any situations or relationships where you recognise that you've collected and stored up angst

2. Think about all the hurt and resentment that you're still storing. This reflection may make you feel uncomfortable or emotional but the end result will be worth it

3. Are any of these thoughts out-of-date or irrelevant? If so, now is an appropriate time to release them. There's no point hanging onto resentment that no longer matters

4. If you've managed to get rid of any of your out-of-date thinking give yourself a pat on the back. This is an achievement worth recognising

5. Thinking about the resentment you're still carrying; what can you do to assertively deal with some of this hurt and resentment? It's no good burying your head in the sand and saying you can't do anything about it. Your choices are i) let it go, ii) be prepared to accept it without fretting about it iii) tackle the issue. The choice is yours

6. Decide what action you're going to take and then create an action plan (including a timescale) and set to work. This may involve speaking to the person who has caused you pain. He/she may be completely unaware of what they've done

7. It's ok to indulge in a little self-pity now and then but you can't allow this to become your natural state as it will erode your self-confidence. Also, this negative state won't fix the problem

8. Ridding yourself of accumulated angst is a real achievement. Don't just dismiss it; reward yourself in some way to mark your success. This is a good self-nurturing technique and will help build your self-confidence

Learning assertiveness skills means you won't end up swinging like a pendulum from passive to aggressive behaviour. This is good news for you and those close to you. Assertive people recognise that others are not responsible for their behaviour. Assertiveness is about taking responsibility for yourself, not blaming other people for your unhappiness.

If someone attacks you emotionally, of course you have every right to feel pain or hurt, just don't hang on to it. Storing angst will simply contaminate your sense of wellbeing and self-confidence. Remember you're in charge of your feelings, and only you can decide how others will affect you.

You may not have the self-confidence to start practicing assertiveness in conflict situations. This is understandable. If this is you, try practicing your assertiveness skills in non-conflict situations first. For example, ask someone to do you a favour or try negotiating a purchase at a car boot sale. These are simple ways to start building your self-confidence.

For completeness here is a brief summary of passive and aggressive behaviour.

Passiveness: Passive behaviour is where you sacrifice your own preferences and needs in favour of someone else's. Of course there will be times in your life when you need to be passive. There may be times when being passive will allow you to build a positive relationship in the long run. The problem arises if passive behaviour becomes your default.

If you're not sure whether you're naturally passive, consider the following:

- Are you constantly seeking approval from other people?
- Do you generally sound uncertain when you're speaking?
- Do you try not to actively participate in discussions or anything that requires standing up for your values?
- Do you constantly belittle your own views? For example, "I'm no expert but...' "I may be wrong but..."
- Are you prone to self-criticism? For example "I'm so stupid..."
- Are you softly spoken? If so, have you always been softly spoken, or is it something else? Is this because you're scared of being heard?
- Do you avoid eye contact?
- Do your facial expressions or body language send out 'discomfort' signals to others?

You don't need to be the life and soul of the party to be naturally confident or assertive. Some of the quietest people can be the most confident. Start to observe the people around you and adopt some of the traits of the confident ones.

Aggressiveness: Aggressive behaviour doesn't always mean physical harm. Aggressive behaviour is any behaviour that causes physical or emotional harm to others. Aggression is not the best approach to getting your own way, and makes relationship building difficult.

If you're not sure if you're naturally aggressive, consider the following:

- Do you resent other people's demands, and make this clear through your words and actions?

- Do you retaliate in a subtle way rather than speaking your mind? This is often referred to as an indirect indication of hostility or passive aggressive
- Do you regularly challenge what other people say, in a somewhat hostile or overpowering manner?
- Do you give the impression of being strong-willed or opinionated? Do you readily share your views about everything?
- Is your default position often no; even before you know what is required?
- Are you dismissive of people who disagree with you?
- Do you find it easy to be argumentative? You may even call this 'having a healthy debate'

There are many different forms of passive and aggressive behaviour. The ones listed above are the traits that most of us recognise. There's plenty of information available about behaviour types if you wish to explore the subject in greater detail.

These are just some of the many characteristics of passive and aggressive behaviour. Stop and consider for a moment - is your default position passive, assertive or aggressive behaviour?

It doesn't matter how you start developing your assertiveness skills. Just get stuck in and see how you get on. Every experience will add to your self-confidence toolkit. No experience is wasted.

Assertiveness and self-confidence sit together very comfortably. The more you're able to behave assertively the greater your self-confidence is likely to be. Here's an opportunity to think about how you may use assertiveness in your life.

Exercise: Assertiveness In Action

Assertiveness skills are useful in every aspect of your life. Assertiveness also builds self-confidence. Self-confidence contributes to a happier and healthier life. Win/win! The nice thing about this exercise is you don't have to try it on a live person. You can test your assertiveness skills on paper first.

You will need a piece of paper and a pen for this exercise.

1. Think of a current situation or relationship that you would like to deal with assertively

2. Write a description of this situation or relationship, and how you feel about it. Write your description is as much detail as possible

3. What would your life be like if this situation/relationship was no longer a problem?

4. Do you care enough about this situation or relationship to do something about it? Would it be wise to do something about it, or will it create more problems? Be completely honest

5. If you decide not to tackle the situation or relationship then you need to change your attitude to it. You need to learn to make the best of the situation. How are you going to learn to accept things as they are?

6. If you decide to tackle this situation or relationship, what are you going to do? Make a list of all the actions you need to take to resolve this situation/relationship

7. Are you ready and willing to take action? Only you will know when you feel strong enough to deal with this situation/relationship

8. On the assumption that you are ready to tackle this situation/relationship we're going to have a practice run. Stand with your feet evenly balanced. Stand up straight, put your shoulders back and hold your head up high. Now allow your arms to hang loosely with your hands open and relaxed

9. Take a few deep breaths to steady your nerves. Try to feel as relaxed as you possibly can

10. Now pretend you're talking to the person you want to tackle. Practice what you want to say. Be aware of your tone of voice. It's important to sound calm and confident

11. You may find a mirror useful for this part of the exercise. This will enable you to monitor your body language and facial expressions as you practice

12. Notice how you feel right now. Remember, this is the new assertive you. How does this feel different to the normal you?

13. As an experiment, now adopt your normal pose (passive or aggressive) and try to convey your message. Notice how different you look and sound

14. Now put yourself in the shoes of the other party. Which of these behaviours are you going to respond to most positively?

15. Are you willing to adopt assertiveness skills, or are you going to stay as you are?

Laughter is another item for your self-confidence toolkit. Even if you're carrying a heavy load, humour can help lighten that load. When people are trying to learn assertiveness skills they sometimes fall into the trap of becoming too serious. Always make room for a little humour in your life.

A laugh or a smile can help diffuse tense situations or remove fear. If you smile or laugh, at the appropriate time, you will appear less confrontational. If you're observant you will notice the other person relax a little. This isn't always immediately obvious so you will need to develop your observation skills.

Visualisation is commonly used for reducing or removing fear. Many coaches and counsellors recommend you find a way to make yourself feel equal to the other party. This can be imagining the other person lacking self-confidence or seeing yourself as a giant and the other person as 'Tom Thumb'.

This is not intended to demean the other person in any way. It's just a coping mechanism to remove your feelings of inadequacy. The point is this person functions in the same way as you do. You're both equal but you need to convince your inner self of this.

You may need to try lots of different things before you find the coping mechanism that works for you. We're all different; what works for one person won't work for someone else.

Laughter and assertiveness really do go hand-in-hand. Assertiveness is a skill worth learning as the long-term benefits outweigh the effort of learning. You may experience some pain on your assertiveness journey but you will be rewarded with greater self-respect and increased self-confidence.

Handling Conflict - Learning to handle conflict well is another really useful skill for your self-confidence toolkit. Knowing you have the self-confidence to deal with conflict situations can remove a lot of misery.

You will find more information about handling conflict and confrontation in chapter 7 'Dealing With Conflict, Confrontation And Bullies'.

As I said at the start of this chapter make self-confidence your new best friend. We all need a few self-confidence tricks from time-to-time. Here are my suggestions for some tricks for your self-confidence toolkit. This list isn't exhaustive. You may have other suggestions of your own.

- There will be times when you don't feel confident, but others perceive you to be confident. Accept their compliments graciously. Also accept that the person they see and hear exists. Develop the respect for yourself that others have for you

- Think back to a time when you felt confident and capable. Visualise the experience as if it's happening right now. Now anchor this feeling so you can recall it whenever you need a quick self-confidence boost

- Being happy will make you feel more self-confident. This is the best kind of self-confidence to have. Get into the habit of noticing the things each day that give you pleasure or make you feel happy. The happier you feel the more confident you will feel

- Keep calm, regardless of the situation. Don't panic if you have a crisis of confidence. Do a mental and physical emergency stop. Take a deep breath, think positively, drop your shoulders, stand up straight and put your brain in gear. Now you're ready to speak or act

- Take time out to monitor your self-confidence periodically. In the initial stages of building self-confidence you may find it helpful to keep a progress diary or journal. This is especially useful if you started your self-confidence journey with major confidence issues

- Motivation is a great tool for building self-confidence. Each time you deal with a situation or experience confidently, make a note of it. This will give you the motivation to rise to the next challenge. To get you started you might like to try the 'My Confidence Over A Week Or Month' Exercise.

Exercise: My Confidence Over a Week or Month

The thing about self-confidence is we rarely notice it growing and developing. It's only when we stop and look back that we discover what an incredible journey we've been on.

Start by monitoring your self-confidence over a week or month. You can continue this exercise if it works for you. I suggest you start by allocating 10 - 15 minutes daily for this exercise.

1. Observe yourself over the next week. Notice when you do things differently, or react to people and situations differently

2. Each day make a note of at least 1 example of your confidence growing. For example, you may have been more relaxed when dealing with a tricky situation. Perhaps you spoke up at a meeting. Did you strike up a conversation with someone you hadn't spoken to before? The possibilities are endless

3. Make a note of what you did. Did you handle the situation how you wanted to? If not, how would you have liked to handle it? What would you do differently if this situation arose again?

4. No matter how big or small these changes are they are an indication that things are changing. It's important to record them so you and monitor your progress

5. At the end of the week/month read your journal. Be very proud of the progress you've made in the last week or month. Allow yourself to savour your achievement

6. Now reward yourself with a treat. This could be a piece of chocolate, me time or something more indulgent. It doesn't matter what the reward is. The important thing is you're telling your brain that you've achieved something and you're feeling very proud

Here are some other things you can practice to build your self-confidence:

- Whenever you walk down the road, into a shop or bar etc, think about how people perceive you. Hold your head up and smile at passers-by. Notice how many respond positively to you.

  We tend to be drawn (unconsciously) to confident people. If you appear confident more people will smile back at you. Notice how this lifts your spirits

- It's often said that failing to plan is planning to fail. Therefore, plan for success. If you have to give a presentation make sure you're properly prepared. You will appear and feel more confident, which gives you a much better chance of success. If you aren't properly prepared it will probably be obvious. This will negatively impact your self-confidence and the outcome

  The same rules apply for job hunting and interviews. Employers will not be impressed with anyone who attends an interview ill-prepared. You're just wasting your time and theirs

- If you have to make a difficult telephone call or deal with a challenging or confrontational matter, stand-up. Stand up straight and hold your head up. This will enable the energy to flow through your body more easily. You will also feel and sound more confident. The other person doesn't need to know that you don't feel confident

- Feel confident in whatever you're wearing. When you wear new clothes do you sometimes feel self-conscious? If so, make friends with your new clothes. Tell yourself you look and feel good. If you enjoy wearing them you will look natural and comfortable, which projects an air of confidence

As your self-confidence grows you will learn to accept that things go wrong sometimes. No-one gets it right all the time. Confident people know and accept this. They accept their successes and failures with equal grace and don't allow either to control them.

Are you willing to make self-confidence your new best friend? I'm sure you've learnt some things you didn't know about yourself as a result of reading 'A Matter of Self-confidence'. This exercise is an opportunity to reflect on your personal self-confidence journey so far.

Exercise: My Self-confidence Success Story

Think about what you've achieved since you started reading this book and analysing your self-confidence. The aim of this exercise is to demonstrate how much self-confidence you've gained.

Do any of these apply to you?

1. I now feel more confident confronting problems instead of running away from them?   Y/N

2. I'm comfortable saying no if something isn't right for me?   Y/N

3. I take responsibility for my own thoughts and actions instead of blaming others?   Y/N

4. I'm a better friend to myself?   Y/N

5. I'm realistic about what I can and can't do, and I accept my limitations? Y/N

6. I'm assertive, rather than passive or aggressive?   Y/N

7. I like myself? I'm becoming more comfortable in my own skin?   Y/N

8. I accept my mistakes, but I don't allow this to hold me back?   Y/N

9. I encourage others to be more confident?   Y/N

10. I've increased my self-confidence toolkit?   Y/N

11. I now understand the difference between self-esteem and self-confidence?   Y/N

12. I'm comfortable making eye contact with people when I greet them? Or, I'm learning to be comfortable making eye contact with people when I greet them?   Y/N

13. My posture and body language sends out a more positive message? Y/N

14. I know and understand myself better now?   Y/N

15. I'm better at taking the initiative?   Y/N

Do you currently have a self-confidence network? If not, now is a good time to establish one. These are the people who lift you up when you're feeling negative (for whatever reason). They will also be people who inspire you or generally make you feel good in some way. Consciously distance yourself from those people who damage your self-confidence.

Remember, only you can give you self-confidence. Your support network will be there to offer support and encouragement when it's needed. Invite the right people into your support network.

"When your self-confidence is low - look back at your life and celebrate your journey so far" - Elizabeth J Tucker

9. My Self-confidence Action Plan

"Always set yourself goals. When you achieve them you will have the self-confidence to move forward" - Elizabeth J Tucker

Self-confidence and achieving your goals are more closely linked than most people realise. How you set your goals and talk about the future will make a significant difference to your self-confidence and achieving your goals. It's about self-belief.

It's worth remembering, great achievements don't always lead to great self-confidence. We often believe that getting a big promotion or winning a major contract will automatically increase our self-confidence. Often this is the case, but not always. Sometimes this quantum leap can leave us feeling insecure and doubting our ability to live up to expectations.

Sustainable self-confidence comes from developing the necessary skills and knowledge, and then having a fundamental belief in yourself. If you're applying for a big promotion or tendering for a major piece of work, do your homework. This will increase your chances of success and your self-confidence.

Whether your aspirations are large or small, you need to set yourself some self-confidence targets. These goals need to be compelling for you. We all respond differently, so what works for you won't work for someone else.

There is no best way to set your goals. What's more there are lots of different ways to set goals for yourself. I've just included three in this book. If these don't work for you, find something that does. Without goals your achievements won't be as great.

Initially you may like to take small steps and actions that build your self-confidence. For example - doing something that scares you. This could be walking into a bar alone or signing up for a leisure activity or workshop. Each challenge will increase your self-confidence.

If goal setting seems a little intimidating or off-putting you might like to start with a goal for the next 24 hours.

Exercise: The Next 24 Hours

Sometimes we can't face setting big or long-term goals. If you're new to goal setting the idea of a big goal may be scary. Either way, here is a very small goal setting exercise that anyone can try.

1. Think of a single thing you could do in the next 24 hours. It needs to be something that will take you outside your comfort zone or stretch you in some way. Perhaps you're going to speak to stranger on the train or bus. Perhaps you're going to make a positive contribution at your next business meeting. The potential options are endless; just do something challenging

2. Decide how you will reward your success. Examples might include buying yourself a small gift, 10 minutes me time, a glass of wine, or anything else you can think of

3. Make a note of how you feel about this task now (before you do it)

4. Keep your promise to yourself and undertake your challenge. Don't make excuses like 'I forgot' or 'lack of time'

5. When you've completed your challenge spend a few minutes reflecting on how you feel. Was it as difficult or challenging as you anticipated? What has it taught you about yourself?

6. Reward your success before you set the next challenge

7. Consider setting some further small challenges. This is a great way to subtly build your self-confidence

Having mastered 24-hour goal setting, now it's time to push yourself a little more. Why not try the 'Self-confidence Ladder' exercise.

Exercise: Self-confidence Ladder

There is no right or wrong way to achieve your self-confidence goals. This is an alternative goal setting exercise. All you need for this exercise is a piece of paper and a pen.

1. On a sheet of paper (A4 is ideal) draw a ladder. Your ladder can have as many rungs as you wish

2. What is your biggest self-confidence challenge? Write this goal on the top rung of your ladder. As this is your biggest challenge it's the one

you're going to tackle last but it's there for you to see each time you look at your ladder

3. Now think of a small, achievable, challenge. This could be something like ringing someone instead of sending an email, or anything else you want to challenge yourself to do. It's important that it stretches you a little or takes you outside your comfort zone. Put this challenge on the first rung of your ladder

4. When do you plan to achieve this goal by? It's important to have a target date. Once you've achieved this goal you need to reward yourself in some way. You could put a gold star on your ladder (next to the challenge) or reward yourself in some other way. Personally, I have a 'shoe fund'. I put £1 in my shoe fund each time I achieve one of my goals. Choose whatever reward works for you

5. Once you've rewarded yourself write your next challenge on the next rung of your ladder. Don't forget to include a target date for this goal

6. Continue to put your challenges (goals) on the ladder and reward yourself each time until you reach your major challenge (goal). Now take a deep breath and know you have the confidence to tackle your biggest challenge too. Write your target date next to this goal before you start

7. When you achieve your big self-confidence challenge (goal) how are you going to reward yourself?

8. Achieve your goal and reward your success

Note: leave your self-confidence ladder somewhere you will see it regularly. This will act as a constant reminder that you're working towards your major self-confidence challenge. It will also demonstrate how much progress you've made so far.

Here's the final goal setting exercise I've included. This exercise takes just five weeks to complete.

Exercise: Notice Your Self-confidence Grow

This exercise should be conducted over a period of five weeks. It doesn't take long; all you need to do is set aside a little time from weeks one to four. On week five you're going to reflect on the changes in you.

1. Week 1 - walk into a room, theatre, bar etc, full of strangers. You don't need to do anything, acknowledge or speak to anyone. Just walk into the room and tell yourself to stay calm. Make a diary or journal note of the

day and what you did. How did you feel doing this? Was it as scary as you expected? Did you feel proud of yourself afterwards?

2. Week 2 - Smile at strangers you meet in the street (or anywhere else) this week. Say hello to at least one stranger this week. Make a diary or journal note of when you did this and how you felt afterwards.

How many people did you smile at and how many responded to you? How many strangers did you have the courage to say hello to? Did everyone you spoke to respond to you?

3. Week 3 - Strike up a conversation with a stranger this week. This can be at work, on the train or bus, at a social gathering, or in any other setting you choose.

This is your toughest challenge so far. Make a diary or journal note of how hard this challenge felt. Were you tempted to skip this challenge? Make a note of your conversation and how you felt before, during and afterwards. Note: It doesn't need to be a lengthy conversation

4. Week 4 - If you rarely contribute in meetings or group conversations, do so at least once this week. Make a diary or journal note. Did you need to psyche yourself up to participate in the discussion or were you comfortable doing this? How did you feel before, during and after the discussion? Were you brave enough to challenge yourself to do this more than once?

5. Week 5 - Review your diary/journal entries and notice the journey you've been on from the start of week one until the end of week four. What's different? How do you feel now? Is there anything that doesn't scare you as much now? Where do you go from here?

Hopefully over the last five weeks you've seen and felt some changes in your self-confidence. I hope you feel enormously proud of yourself. Often it's much easier to stay in a comfortable rut than step outside your comfort zone.

It took courage to make a conscious decision to tackle your self-confidence issues. Almost certainly you've stepped outside your comfort zone over the last few weeks. How do you feel now? Has this inspired you to keep going on your self-confidence journey?

Procrastination is the enemy of self-confidence. To quote Norman Peale *"action is a great restorer and builder of confidence"*. Don't let lack of self-confidence stop you enjoying all the things life has to offer you.

"What could we accomplish if we knew we could not fail?" - Eleanor Roosevelt

10. Conclusion

"Self-confidence is not a feeling of superiority, but of independence" -
Lama Yeshe

Congratulations! You've done all the hard work and now you get to acknowledge how far you've come. Recognise every accomplishment, large and small, since your started your self-confidence journey. This not only keeps you motivated, it builds self-esteem, which is vital to sustainable self-confidence.

Make a list of five accomplishments that you can celebrate as a result of your new self-confidence:

1.

2.

3.

4.

5.

Now celebrate by giving yourself a treat for each one.

Being confident is a very grown-up act. It means there are no hiding places where you can blame others for your situation. It's also very empowering as it gives you control over your life. Taking responsibility for your own thoughts and actions will allow you to be the driver, not a passenger, in your life journey.

I would love everyone to have more self-confidence. It really does help create a deep sense of wellbeing. I'm convinced that once you get a taste of growing self-confidence you will want more. You won't want to return to your old ways.

Self-confidence is like every other personal development goal; it's a journey not a destination. I hope your self-confidence journey just gets better and better for you. The greater your self-confidence the more opportunities life will give you.

There are probably lots of things you need to know about self-confidence. I've picked five things that I believe everyone should know:

- No matter how unkind other people's words are you are the one who chooses to accept them. Therefore, your lack of self-confidence is down to you
- Part of being confident involves investing in other people's lives. Giving something back or paying something forward is a wonderful way to increase your self-confidence. This is largely due to the sense of fulfilment you feel
- Arrogance is not the same thing as self-confidence. Self-confidence doesn't involve ramming your opinions or virtuous deeds down other people's throats. Self-confidence is about letting others know how good you are and then allowing them to praise your virtues
- If you're genuinely confident you don't need to tell the world. Conduct yourself confidently and others will see and feel the presence you create
- People respond to how you present yourself. It doesn't matter whether you feel confident or not. If others perceive you to be confident they will respond to this. A little fake self-confidence won't harm anyone

Decide what you're going to do with the rest of your life. No matter what your age is, change is constant. How you deal with life's changes will develop or crush your self-confidence. I hope you'll choose the positive option.

To help you on your self-confidence journey I've created a nine-step guide to a more confident you. The easiest way to develop sustainable self-confidence is in manageable chunks. Learn step-by-step how to consciously increase your self-confidence level.

Only you know what your desired level of self-confidence is. Use this framework to assess your current self-confidence level and how to get where you want to be. Begin building your self-confidence today so you can have the life you want and deserve!

Step 1 - Understand what self-confidence is and is not. Until you understand what self-confidence is and where you are on the confidence scale it's virtually impossible to do anything about it. It's a bit like trying to build a house without any foundations

Step 2 - Decide what your desire, decision and commitment is. In order to build self-confidence, you need to decide this is what you want. Next, consider the benefits of greater self-confidence for you personally. Where in your life are you already confident? Where do you need to increase your self-confidence?

Make a list of where you want to start, and pick one thing to do today. Every achievement has to start with a commitment to do something. It's impossible to deal with every self-confidence issue at once, which is why I suggest you pick just one thing

Step 3 - Who you are and who you want to be? Think about your strengths, vulnerabilities, dreams and fears. To be truly confident you need to believe in yourself and be able to appreciate all your qualities. If you find this hard to do; imagine you're deciding this on behalf of someone else looking at you.

Make a list of your attributes. It's important to make sure you have a 'pro' for every 'con' you list. Enlist the help of the people who matter most to you. Ask them what's special about you. It's important to accept their feedback graciously and believe them!

Step 4 - Ditch your self-limiting beliefs and shift to empowering beliefs instead. Be prepared; this stage may take some time. The key is to just get started - procrastination severely hampers personal development.

Consider how you see, think about and talk to yourself. The chances are you're kinder to other people than you are to yourself. Negative thoughts and comments need to be reframed into something positive. That doesn't mean you need to be perfect or pretend a tough situation is good. It means you're taking responsibility for yourself and your life.

Be willing to accept your strengths and vulnerabilities equally. Make a list of some of your self-limiting beliefs and ways you can reframe them to serve you better. Work towards your new beliefs

Step 5 - Now you've put the foundations in place you can move onto the fun part, and develop the self-confidence you desire. Develop the courage to step outside your comfort zone and overcome your fears. Know that self-confidence is waiting on the other side of your fears.

Do things that make you feel confident and do them often. Start with the easy stuff and work your way up to the big stuff. Remember, self-confidence is like any other skill; you develop it with regular practice. If this feels scary, start with something you're already good at and get better at it. When you feel ready, move onto new activities

Step 6 - Celebrate your progress, accomplishments and efforts. You've done all the hard work and now it's time to acknowledge how far you've come. Spend a little time savouring your success.

Recognising your achievements will keep you motivated and build your self-esteem, which is vital to maintaining self-confidence. Make a list of five achievements that you can celebrate now. Reward yourself by giving yourself a treat for each one

Step 7 - Don't stop now. Keep building on your successes. Like any emotion, self-confidence has its ebb and flow moments. As your self-confidence develops and begins to play a bigger role in your life, the challenges may get bigger as well. The difference is you will feel more able to deal with these challenges.

Step 8 - Maintain high levels of self-confidence and self-esteem in the same way you maintain a healthy body. Do it with thoughtful and consistent positive action.

Step 9 - Remember to recharge your self-confidence batteries regularly. Make a list of five actions you can take and pick one to do today.

And so to my final thought on self-confidence... the only person in control of you is you. When you lacked self-confidence you probably blamed it on other people. When you're genuinely confident you recognise that you control your thoughts, feelings and beliefs. In short, your self-confidence is down to you and no-one else.

You weren't born with low self-confidence; it took time and effort to get to this point. Therefore, it makes sense that your journey to a high level of self-confidence will also take time. Be very proud of the progress you have made so far!

If you have a story to share, please do get in touch. My email address is shepherdcreativelearning@gmail.com.

If you're interested in our self-confidence home study programmes please look at our website www.shepherdcreativelearning.co.uk or get in touch via email - shepherdcreativelearning@gmail.com

I hope your self-confidence just keeps on developing. I'm sure life will provide you with lots of exciting opportunities; you just need to spot them.

Do you feel inspired to make friends with self-confidence now? It really is one of the best gifts you could ever give yourself.

If you would like to share your self-confidence story or observations please do get in touch - shepherdcreativelearning@gmail.com.

Thank you for buying my book and allowing me to be a small part of your personal journey. I hope in some small way I've made a difference.

"Practice, practice, practice. The more you do something the more your self-confidence will grow" - Elizabeth J Tucker

Happy confidence building!

11. Appendices

In the Appendices section I have included some common terms used when discussing self-confidence. I've also included some affirmations to get you started and a self-confidence progress log.

Terms and Definitions

There are lots of terms used when discussing self-confidence. I thought you might find it helpful to have a list of the most commonly used terms and their definition:

Arrogance - this involves believing you're better at something than you are. For arrogant people being right is more important than being capable

Ego - the dictionary defines this as the opinion that you have about yourself. According to Freud your ego prevents you from acting on your basic urges, but also works to achieve a balance with your moral and idealistic standards

Low self-esteem - this involves believing you're less valuable than you are

Morale - is about your feelings of enthusiasm and loyalty regarding a task or job. Morale is sometimes used for describing groups as well as individuals

Narcissism - this is about craving admiration from others. This is also often demonstrated by extreme selfishness and lack of empathy with others

Overconfidence - this may be a front for lack of self-confidence. Overconfidence often appears to others as arrogance or cockiness. Scratch the surface and find out what lies beneath

Self-assurance - is confidence in the validity and value of your own ideas and opinions

Self-centred - much like narcissism, this is limited to caring only about yourself and your own needs

Self-confidence - this involves knowing what you're good at and the value you provide. This is not arrogance as you have a healthy and honest opinion of what you're good at and what you're not good at

Self-esteem - in psychology, the term self-esteem is used to describe your overall sense of self-worth or personal value. Self-esteem can involve a variety of beliefs about yourself, such as your appearance, beliefs, emotions, and behaviours

Self-possession - this describes your control over your emotions or reactions, especially when under stress

Self-regard - the dictionary describes this as the quality of being worthy of esteem or respect

Self-respect - this means respecting yourself above all else. If you don't respect yourself it's unlikely that you will receive respect from other people

Self-worth - the dictionary defines self-worth as "the sense of one's own value or worth as a person"

The Dunning-Kruger effect - this is where unskilled individuals suffer from illusory superiority. As you're reading this book I suspect this is not an issue for you

Vanity - this is the excessive belief in your own abilities or attractiveness to others

Exercise: Affirmations

Affirmations are short powerful statements. Like mantras, affirmations have a role to play in all aspects of your life. One of the wonderful things about affirmations is you can use them wherever and whenever you wish.

1. Why not challenge yourself to create your own personal set of affirmations. These are the personal messages that will help build your self-confidence. Here are some affirmations to get you started:

- I am amazing as I am
- I am becoming more confident by caring for myself and learning strategies to grow my self-confidence
- I am proud of all my achievements - big and small
- I am special with every single cell in my body
- I am surrounded by very lovely and genuine friends who only wish the best for me. For my part - I'm a good friend too
- I am unique
- I am what I am and that's ok
- I can do anything that I set my mind to do
- I feel positive energy running through my entire body
- If I truly want something I will achieve it
- I have released my fears and now accept that as I successfully overcome my challenges so my self-confidence grows

- I have the self-confidence to achieve whatever I want to achieve. I recognise that my world is only limited by my own imagination
- I just get better and more confident every day. I use my new self-confidence to help others who are less confident than me
- I like myself as I am
- I'm a beautiful confident human being, who embraces my strengths and weaknesses equally
- I'm confident in my abilities
- I'm great as I am and don't need to change to please others
- I no longer need to feel anxious as I know I'm good enough as I am
- I will put all my strength in my actions, and I will break any obstacle that may rise
- There is no-one and nothing that can stop me achieving my goals

2. Repeat your affirmation (positive message) in your head as often as you wish. You should do this several times a day, every day until you truly the believe the messages you're saying or thinking

Exercise: My Self-confidence Progress Log

Identifying when your confidence grows is an essential part of speeding up the process of increased self-confidence. The more aware you become of your growing self-confidence the more confident you will become, and so the cycle continues.

1. Before you start your self-confidence journey it's important to identify your current confidence level. Otherwise it will be impossible for you to notice how well you're doing.

At the end of the exercise instructions you will find a 12-week chart, which will enable you to plot your progress.

2. When you're ready put a cross in the relevant box on the 'Before' line. This is your self-confidence level before you begin working to increase it. For example - you might feel your current confidence level is 4

3. Each week spend a few minutes reflecting on how you feel. Notice how you feel about yourself, your skills and your self-confidence. Put a cross in the relevant box for that week

4. At the end of week 12 look at your chart and notice the progress you've made. Even the smallest increase in self-confidence is a big step forward

5. Don't forget to reward your success at the end of week 12 as this will help to keep you motivated. It also tells your brain that you're doing something positive

	0 (low)	1	2	3	4	5	6	7	8	9	10
Week 12											
Week 11											
Week 10											
Week 9											
Week 8											
Week 7											
Week 6											
Week 5											
Week 4											
Week 3											
Week 2											
Week 1											
Before											
	0 (low)	1	2	3	4	5	6	7	8	9	10

Success starts with self-confidence!

www.ingramcontent.com/pod-product-compliance
Lightning Source LLC
Chambersburg PA
CBHW072229050426
42443CB00032B/725